December Sky

Beyond My Undocumented Life

For my mother, Rosario,
Whose sacrifice is my inspiration

For my father, Juan Antonio,
Whose love is one of my most cherished blessings

For my daughter, Dakota Xochitl,
Who has shown me the meaning of it all

And for my dear nephews and nieces,
Frank, Neiko, Steven, Jesse, Bryan, Alex, Christopher,
Andrea, Khiobon, Abeline, and Josué, and my cousins
born in the United States and other far-away places,
Who motivated me to remember in the first place

❧❧❧❧❧❧❧❧❧❧❧❧❧❧❧❧❧❧❧❧❧❧❧❧❧❧❧❧❧❧❧❧

Para mi Madre, Rosario,
Cuyo sacrificio es mi inspiración

Para mi padre, Juan Antonio,
Cuyo amor es una de mis mayores bendiciones

Para mi Hija, Dakota Xochitl,
Quien me ha demonstrado el significado de todo

Y para mis queridos sobrinos,
Frank, Neiko, Steven, Jesse, Bryan, Alex, Christopher,
Andrea, Khiobon, Abeline, y Josué, y mis primos
nacidos en los Estados Unidos y otros lugares lejanos,
Quienes me motivaron a recordar en el principio

December Sky

Beyond My Undocumented Life

Evelyn Cortez-Davis

Author Photograph by Troy Jévon Davis

Cover photograph "The Farewell – Rosario & Evelyn"
© 1973 by Juan Antonio Cortez

Cover and "In Xochitl In Cuicatl" logo design by **Moonlight Creative Works**

Published in 2005 by
In Xochitl In Cuicatl Productions

P.O. Box 295
Altadena CA 91003-0295
IXICpress@gmail.com

Printed and distributed by CafePress.com
in the United States of America

To order more copies, visit **www.cafepress.com/ecdavis**
or call (877) 809-1659 (Product Number 21351652)

ISBN-10: 0-9768382-0-6
ISBN-13: 978-0-9768382-0-3   v. 3 (2008-11)

CONTENTS

STORMS

It was six in the morning on that clear December day. The crisp air chilled my hands as I walked with my mom and my three sisters to the taxicab parked outside our house. This moment marked the beginning of our new life.

The sound of my father and the cab driver loading our luggage into the trunk bounced off the countless rows of tract houses in my sleeping neighborhood. My sisters and I piled up in the back seat. I looked through the taxicab window and I noticed the bright orange sun rising over the *Duralita* rooftops. A million things might have crossed my mind at that instant. Perhaps that the cab was far too small to hold my entire family. Or how unfortunate it was that my parents could not afford for my father to travel with us until later. In fact, the excitement of our destination alone should have been enough to keep my mind occupied. I was only twelve years old, but I had spent most of my life waiting. I waited for the day that Mom would return from working in the United States and stay for good. At least, I had hoped that if she ever had to leave again that she would take us with her, and as I waited with my sisters in that taxicab, my wish was coming true. Yet, at the time, a sudden realization kept me hypnotized: that I might not get to see the sun rise over those rooftops again. The finality of this trip hit me all at once. My parents had spent weeks coaching us and we had many loving relatives awaiting us in Los Angeles, but leaving El Salvador for good was not easy in the least.

After our bags were loaded, the driver took the crowded taxi through our suburban town of Soyapango. It took about half an hour to reach the bus station in downtown San Salvador. Once we arrived, the six of us emerged from the cab and waited for a few minutes to board the charter bus that would take us to Guatemala City. Saying good-bye to Papi burned a hole through my heart, but I found comfort in knowing that he would soon join us. My oldest sister, Sonia, hugged him first, then Milady, and then it was my turn, followed by Daysi. We always tended to do important things in order of age, as though it were more formal this way. One by one, we got on the bus. The bus had a heavy and distinct new vinyl smell, as if the seats had been just reupholstered, but we soon got used to it. We found two seats side by side and a third one in the row right behind. I placed my small bag next to Milady's. Sonia found her place behind us next to a young man we did not know. Daysi sat alone on the right waiting for Mom. The other passengers quickly filled the bus. My father tried hopelessly to smile at us as we peered through the tinted windows but there was an obvious and overwhelming sadness in his eyes. Mom was the last person to board the bus. She stalled until the last possible moment, since her brother, Carlos, was on his way to see us off. Tío Carlos had been a constant presence in my life and my sisters' since birth. It would be truly disheartening not to see him before we left.

After a few moments, she hung her head down and climbed on. The driver slammed the doors shut behind her. She sat down on the empty seat next to Daysi and slowly looked over her shoulder as the bus pulled away. She stood from her seat when she noticed her brother running on the sidewalk toward the door. When I looked back, I saw Tío Carlos, waving his hands in the air, trying to catch us. My father stood at the station door with a solid frown and his arms crossed. Papi got farther away by the second as my uncle ran. The bus did not stop. I looked at Mami as she sat back down. She did not bother to wipe away the tears. Perhaps she had not noticed them, as I had not noticed my own. It was obvious to me that this trip would change our lives forever. We had not yet left and my life had changed already.

As we got on our way, I fidgeted in my seat trying to doze off, leaning on my sister's shoulder. All along I knew the knot in my throat was too huge to ever let me sleep. Daysi did the same, trying to go to sleep without getting entangled in mom's long hair. The brown tinted windows of the bus were not dark enough to block out the sun from my wide eyes, so I stared outside. I stared out the window as we rode eastward through the many small towns on the way to the Guatemalan border. The old houses on the narrow avenues overflowed with character. Without words, the little houses told stories of the heat and of thunder, of harvests and of hunger, of the joy and of the grief of the farm worker. The stories were simple, yet far too intricate for my young ears. The paint peeling off the thick adobe walls fought a brave battle against the sun and time. Between towns, I counted the numbers on the signs announcing the kilometers by the road. The ever-decreasing numbers told me the distance remaining from the border. I struggled not to hear the deafening silence of Mami and my sisters. It was very typical of Mami to keep her feelings inside. She only spoke once.

"Look outside and remember what you see," she said.

She knew we might not return for a very long time and hoped we could stay connected to our home somehow. This was her way of ensuring that the speeding bus did not yank our roots from underneath us. I do recall trying to do as Mami said, but sadly, my most vivid memory of the first few hours on the bus is the smell of the vinyl seats.

There was nothing particularly engaging about this bus ride. A few hours later, we approached a wire fence and a small building at the top of a hill, which I could only assume was the borderline. The bus stopped briefly while the driver checked in at the border gates at *Valle Nuevo, Juliapa*. The midday sun had managed to chase away the morning chill from the landscape. Dozens of food vendors gathered around the buses passing through, hoping to scrape together a living by selling morsels to the passengers.

From my seat on the sunny side of the bus, I watched the vendors circle the bus chanting eagerly. They held up plates of *riguas, totopostes,* sizzling *chicharrones*, handmade tortillas, cold *gaseosa* bottles, and gigantic plantain *empanadas* with sugar sprinkles that danced in the sun. Although most of it looked tempting, I knew Mami never liked buying us food from street vendors. "Too many germs," she always said, so I did not bother asking. The loudness of the chants rose to near screams as the driver made his way back. Our stop was short and soon the bus continued into Guatemala, kicking up a trail of dust behind us. I had no idea how I could think of food at all. The knot in my throat was barely beginning to subside.

We arrived at the bus station in Downtown Guatemala City around noon. I had never been to another country before. We had only enough time to eat a small lunch at the station. My mother, my three sisters, and I, sat silently around a small table on the second floor, overlooking the empty lobby. I finally began to think ahead and to get excited about our trip. Soon enough, we saw the bus pull up on the street just outside the double glass doors below. While my sisters and I boarded the bus, Mami made sure our few bags were loaded, and we were on our way again. We did not bring much. We packed just enough clothes for a two week trip, should it last that long. Mami was careful to pack shampoo and soap and other toiletries she had brought with her from the U.S. one month earlier so we would appear more like tourists on our way through Mexico. We removed clothing labels, luggage markings, and brand names from everything we packed. We even burnt off the well-known *Bracos* name from the soles and the sides of our new tennis shoes. Mami thought of everything — there was no room for mistakes. Once in our second shuttle, we assumed the same seating arrangement again. The young man who had sat next to Sonia on the first bus, Víctor, sat next to her again. He was apparently following the same route. He tried hopelessly to engage her in his flirtatious conversation. Milady and I found this highly entertaining, as we blatantly eavesdropped from our seat in front of them.

Soon enough, I lost interest in the conversation behind me, and I looked out the window. It was a perfectly gorgeous afternoon. The air seemed as clean as it could be, like right after a heavy rain. There were a few perfect cotton puff clouds scattered about. After leaving the rush and noise of the city, the sun lit up the mountains and a perfect sapphire sky. With my mind focused on the surroundings, the same feeling that overwhelmed me at sunrise that morning grabbed a hold of me again. We were leaving the only home I ever knew. It was where I kept everything that was mine: my family, my friends, and my memories. Memories of outings and games, of summers and holidays, of legends and of family. My happy and carefree childhood ended up in the hasty maturity shared by many Central American children my age. The harsh memories know little of distance or time and they will remain with me forever.

The clearest of these memories goes back to an afternoon about a year and a half earlier. It seems as if it was yesterday. It all began as a normal day, in the humid San Salvador heat. Despite my teacher's blank stare out the open window, all the girls in my sixth grade class worked silently on their math exams with commendable discipline and restraint. I answered the last question, sighed as I put down my pencil, and quietly took my paper to the teacher's desk. My older sister, Milady, smiled at me as I walked away... she was surely almost finished with the test as well. I stepped softly out of the room to join my two friends who also finished early.

With our exam completed and only an hour left in the school day, we felt exhilarated. The three of us ran giggling down the hall to look at the boys in the private school next door. The white handkerchiefs pinned to the lapels of our red and white uniforms were immobile as we dashed down the hall. The tiny Leonardo Azcunaga Elementary School for Girls had no eyes to the outside except at the end of that very hallway. Not even my oldest sister Sonia's school, the Albert Einstein Private Institute to our right, had the privilege of such privacy. A two-story building housed all our classrooms and wrapped around the courtyard. The wall enclosing the rest of the yard completed the fortress effect. The huge *almendro* tree sat in front of the outdoor stage, covering the schoolyard with shade, invisible to the outside world. Every day that we spent within these walls, life went on unnoticed outside. Our campus was located on Soyapango's main street,

Roosevelt Boulevard. The commercial heart of town was found East of our school on the boulevard, which was lined with liquor stores, dry cleaners, merchant-owned homes, a dozen or so tiny public and private schools, and at least twice that many abandoned structures, destroyed by bombs or fires. West along the main street, the area was residential, with the local cemetery as the eerie borderline just a few blocks from our school. The graveyard was just far enough not to be noticed from the second-floor balcony at the end of the hallway, where my friends and I awaited the bell to go home.

As we stood enjoying our window to the world outside, we heard the all-too-familiar sound of gunshots quickly approaching. We looked over the balcony to the right, looking for reactions from the neighbors standing close by. A woman rushed to shut her windows and her front door. My friends watched the students of the school next door quickly abandon the yard. We panicked and raced to our classroom to bring our teacher the bad news.

"They're shooting! They're shooting!" my friends and I whispered to our teacher as softly as we could, but we caught the attention of the entire class anyway. We knew we were in trouble. We were trained to drop to the floor and take cover as soon as blasts were heard. We knew to always be home before the seven o'clock civilian curfew imposed by the military. We knew much about the precautions, but nothing of the reasons. Milady and my younger sister Daysi who attended the Azcunaga School with me, both knew to always be prepared for anything. But I stayed put, waiting for the teacher to react. "It's just firecrackers," he reassured the class, "now finish your tests."

We took our seats, with our eyes fixed on the open windows, convinced that there could not be fireworks that powerful. Seconds dragged into minutes after he dismissed our announcement. Eventually, the violent noise of blasting and shooting grew so close that he was forced to acknowledge the danger. The roar of a helicopter drew nearer and nearer by the second. Then it came. The military chopper was suspended dangerously close to our classroom window, fluttering. Its unmistakable outline contrasted sharply against the fluorescent blue sky behind it. One of the soldiers was leaning partly out of the door-less helicopter. He seemed young, even to me, he couldn't have been older than sixteen. The machine gun he held tightly against his camouflaged uniform probably weighed more than he did. The chopper hovered as though searching for something or someone below. Our teacher finally decided we should evacuate the second floor. We quickly formed a single file, and I grabbed onto Milady's hand to make sure we were not separated. We lowered ourselves to our hands and knees, and led by our teacher, crawled slowly to the staircase. The red and white checkers on my uniform turned brown with dirt as we dragged along the floor. I could hear the helicopter above us but I did not dare look. I could hear the nervous whispers of my classmates, wondering what would happen to us, where we were headed, and when we could all go home. The same hallway that I walked in seconds every day stretched for miles that afternoon. At the top of the stairs, we stood up and the teacher rushed us down to the most remote room on the first floor, where the rest of the school was being rounded up.

The windows of the classroom were covered by the thick shade of the trees in the school's garden. One by one, each class was brought to the dim room. It felt as though hours passed before my sister Daysi's fourth grade class arrived and the three of us were finally together. Later, as the last group was being brought in, gunshots exploded right outside our gate. The younger girls whimpered. My sixth grade class, the oldest students in the school, tried helplessly to comfort them. Meanwhile, the teachers attempted to compile a plan of action. The Principal told us that the national guardsmen in the helicopter we had seen earlier had confronted *guerrilla* forces surrounding our school, leaving us trapped in the middle...and now the only thing left to do was wait. Although Mami was thousands of miles away working in the U.S. at that time, her presence was there with us. She reminded my sisters and me of the single most important thing that she taught us to do in times of need: pray. So, my sisters and I gathered a few of our classmates around us and broke the tension in the room with a simple prayer.

By five o'clock, the helicopter had retreated and the shooting had slowly moved away from our campus. However, the Principal announced that no one would be released from the school until a guardian came to take them home. My sisters and I immediately realized that if my dad got home before us, he would surely come find us despite the shooting, despite the military curfew, or any other type of danger involved. We were determined to get home before he did. We prayed for a miracle. Just then, the mother of our friend Ruby arrived to take her home, only a couple of blocks from our house. Our miracle. We begged Ruby's mom to take us home, as did at least ten other girls who lived nearby. For better or for worse, she decided to take us all. We did not witness anyone at our school getting shot, but we were more than relieved to leave. We clung to each other while we could and, leaving our books behind, we started our three-mile trek home.

The afternoon sun had retreated into the clouds of an oncoming storm. Although the shooting had temporarily subsided, mass hysteria continued around us. The people on the sidewalks were still frantic, taking shelter wherever they found an open door: stores, buildings, schools, homes...We unclipped the handkerchiefs from our uniforms. The white cloth would signal to others that we were not involved in the violence, only caught up in it. We bit on one corner to hang them visibly from our mouths and raised our empty hands toward the gray sky.

Ruby's mom took us the long way home, through the commercial part of town, since she had heard that the faster route past the cemetery was too dangerous. We walked East along the Boulevard past the closed stores and homes. Even the few abandoned, half-demolished buildings along the boulevard had boards propped over the decaying doorways. Our heads were moist with the drizzle that started its way down. In about twenty minutes, we reached the boulevard going north to Tonacatepeque. We were less than an hour's walk away from home. An occasional stroke of lightning lit up the skies every few minutes. In the blink of an eye, the light mist turned into heavy rain, drenching every inch of us.

Dozens of people walked along this route, with their arms suspended above their heads. Traffic was always heavy along this road, even on that day. There were a few stores at each intersection, closed, of course. The busy commercial street eventually turned into a highway of sorts. Its lack of sidewalks reminded us that it was not meant for pedestrians. The muddy right shoulder would have to be good enough for us. The rain, washing away the hill that the road cut through, created a muddy current against our feet.

My wet arms were cold and began to feel numb from being raised for so long. The multiple layers of my cotton uniform had fused together into a heavy, dripping mess. My socks were unbearably wet and my shoes made an annoying sloshing sound with every step. We came upon a huge pile of wet trash against the hillside covering our walkway. We had actually walked into the pungent odor about half a block back. Carefully watching the cars on our left, Ruby's mom led the girls one by one onto the paved road to get around it. My sisters and I waited at the back of the group with our handkerchiefs still securely gripped between our teeth. Other bystanders impatiently rushed past us on the slick asphalt, ignoring the traffic still honking past us at full speed. It continued to pour.

Just beyond the blocked shoulder, a small road intersecting the boulevard marked the site of a small liquor store on our left. I squinted to look through the heavy rain at some guards standing in the store's parking lot, leaning on their military truck. They seemed disinterested in our dilemma and just stood around with their weapons rested against their hips. Just before the smell of the rotting trash knocked me to my knees, I realized all the girls had made it over except for my sisters and me. When it was Daysi's turn to be helped across, a machine gun was fired somewhere close by. The shots were so close that the sound pierced loudly through my eardrums and triggered the soldiers down the street into a shooting frenzy. Commotion seized the street all over again. People ran in all directions seeking refuge. Ruby's mom took her group and ran away to safety without looking back. She had done the best she could to help us. Unable to get past the obstacle course of fleeing cars and puddles of mud and piles of garbage to catch up to them, Milady grabbed my hand and Daysi's and ran the other way. We were on our own.

We ran back with a crowd of people who had been walking behind us. We quickly retraced our steps along the boulevard, desperately searching for shelter from the bullets, finding nothing. The loudness of the gunfire was alarming, because no matter how far we ran, it did not seem to fade. Eventually, we spotted a pharmacy a few blocks back, on a hopelessly unprotected corner. Although the pharmacy was closed and did not appear safe, there was a large number of people standing against its wall, waiting. So we stood there, trembling against the wet wall. Daysi and I sobbed uncontrollably, but I'll never forget Milady's strength. She did not shed a single tear. At eleven years old she was responsible for us and would not let us down.

That is when she came. Since then I have always believed she was our guardian angel, but in the confusion of that fateful day, she was nothing but a stranger. A woman approached us and asked if we were alone. She must have been in her early thirties. She spoke softly and was dressed modestly. Realizing our obvious reluctance to answer, she added that she was just trying to get home herself. Her comforting voice finally convinced us it was safe to trust her. She offered to stand beside us so we would not be alone and we eventually agreed. In the minutes that followed, the rain eased down and the shots faded until they were almost silent. Once other people began to move on, our lady friend promised to walk with us the rest of the way. And so we went on for a couple of miles with our arms still raised amidst a crowd, which seemed to have grown to hundreds.

They were students, teachers, food vendors, construction workers, men, women, and children of all ages. We turned into the main street of Los Santos, our neighborhood, quite far from the soldiers and the bullets, but not far enough. I was not wearing a watch, but it was clearly dusk and I had a feeling that our delay at the pharmacy had prevented us from getting home before Dad. Our arms were still raised and our tiny jaws were fixed in place, still gripping those handkerchiefs over our chins. Our companion assured us it was safe to relax. She left us around the corner from our house and continued her own way home. She hurried her pace, rapidly disappearing into the gray of the evening, taking her name with her. No matter how hard I tried, I could not remember her name. We never saw her again.

The three of us stormed into the house to find our sister Sonia pacing, sick with worry. She had heard the news on the radio of the shooting in town. Papi had arrived home half an hour earlier. As we expected, he had left immediately to go find us. We prayed that he would be turned away from the area, as the seven o'clock curfew was dangerously near, and soldiers had blocked off most roads. We worried that the umbrellas he took to protect us from the rain gave the impression of weapons in the distance. Again, there was nothing left to do but wait. He returned home soon later, turned back by soldiers at the edge of town. When I saw the despair in his face disappear, I finally felt safe.

My sister's courage, my father's conviction, my mother's teachings, a young woman's compassion— they all remain as vivid as that gloomy afternoon, clinging to my memory like the smell of wet earth after the storm.

As we traversed the Guatemalan countryside in our charter bus, I got farther and farther from those places but not from the feelings. There, in my seat on the sunny side of the bus, the urge to sleep won me over. The knot in my throat had completely vanished and I slept soundly. I leaned my head on my sister's shoulder as her head rested on top of mine. Somehow or other, I was sure that the troubles of the war that surrounded us in the recent years would remain in the past, like echoes in the distance.

ECHOES

"THE PEOPLE — UNITED — WILL NEVER BE DEFEATED!"

Five armed guerrilleros took over my elementary school for an afternoon in 1980. Their shouts bounced in unison against the walls of our school fortress. Schools were often "overthrown" by guerrilleros this way to expose the students to their message and to defy local authorities.

Their young faces were covered with red bandanas. They ordered each class onto the courtyard and lined us all up in single files. They paced up and down the aisles of red and white uniforms, seemingly proud of their military superiority over grade school girls. One of them stood over us leaning over the railing of the second floor and addressed us as though we could comprehend his message. We were forced to hold up our left arms and raise our tiny fists in countless moments of silence for the dead of the war. They proceeded to chant in support of their comrades in battle, expecting us to follow along.

"EL PUEBLO — UNIDO — JAMAS SERA VENCIDO!"

They kept us there for an eternity. They eventually retreated before the military showed up. That day I realized that children were not immune from the pressures of war. No one was.

I knew little about the turmoil around us then. The civil war I witnessed between peasants-turned-soldiers and El Salvador's military forces began long before my time. They fought over land reform and social equity. The fight, however noble at the beginning, deteriorated along the way into something less than noble. As kids, all we needed to know was not to ask questions or make comments about either side, especially in public. This restriction was constant and unspoken. We knew that talking about the political situation was commonly misconstrued as choosing a side, which always meant choosing the wrong side. We learned at a young age that "subversive" behavior was wrong. We also learned that criticism of the government in any form was considered subversive. If I had been granted the privilege of outspoken curiosity, I would not have known what to ask. I knew very little... that was the way things were supposed to be. It was impossible to distinguish between the right and the wrong side. I understood that each side was capable of murdering those who disagreed with them.

In my parents' eyes, the guerrilla was a business venture, surging out of the struggle to make a living. According to my parents, the guerrilleros treated the war as a job rather than as a struggle against oppression. Mom and Dad believed that the fighting was unnecessary, that they had ways to move ahead without war. Most strikingly, despite the constant violence around us, my parents were never interested or even curious about politics. Like most of their peers, my parents kept themselves distanced and disconnected, choosing to focus their energies on supporting the family and remaining "productive."

We heard one alarming rumor after another. I heard of the military's bus searches to locate suspicious people for questioning. The suspects were seldom seen alive again. I learned about the many people arrested by the military, taken from their homes, their jobs, from buses, from the street. Circling vultures were often the only clue revealing countryside ravines where their bodies turned up. We heard from a classmate about the corpse of a young pregnant girl dumped in a cemetery. She had been shot in the chest and was found next to her boyfriend's headless body. Their clothes were completely soaked in blood. When her hysterical parents insisted she was not pregnant and demanded an examination, horrified police found, inserted in her stomach, the boy's severed head.

The cemetery by my school, like most other urban graveyards, became a corpse depository. Most days, I preferred crossing the street to avoid walking by the cemetery entrance on my way to school. The putrid smell and the unmistakable crowd of nosy onlookers would tell of yet another corpse that was discovered, probably shot at point blank range and dumped on the grounds in the middle of the night. Daysi and her friends did not cross the street one day, and unknowingly walked right past a decomposing body that had been dumped at the gates. She had nightmares about this gory encounter for many nights. Images of the blistered, rotting skin she described snuck into my mind too, even though I never saw it myself.

The torture of prisoners by the National Guard was no rumor. Men and women were beaten, often to death, for confessions of their connection to the so-called "subversives." My dad's youngest brother, Tío Pedro, was one of the unfortunate ones. Guerrilla "recruiters", who happened to be union organizers at the time, approached him to join the movement. They wanted to bring him along on a mission to block some major roads, by stopping and burning up any buses that drove by. This would delay the guards' access to certain areas of strategic significance for the "movement." My uncle refused. After this, his troubles with the military began. He had been anonymously and falsely reported as a guerrillero to the authorities. The National Guard arrested him, but no one was notified. He simply vanished.

My dad and his sister, Tía Carmen, were twice asked to identify bodies found on roadsides outside of town. In the meantime, Tío Pedro endured beatings by the guards for many days. They accused him of "subversive" activity, including the burning of buses that he had refused to be involved in. He proclaimed his innocence and refused to sign a confession. He was told that if he identified his other subversive "friends," he would receive a full pardon and be set free. Severely beaten and desperate for relief, he reluctantly agreed to cooperate. He was driven to the gate of the IUSA factory where my father worked. There, he pointed out the IUSA workers who had tried to recruit him. Tío Pedro gasped as he saw my father leaving for the day, praying he would not look his way and recognize him. He was still missing at the time.

Tío Pedro had fulfilled his part of the deal, but his captors had lied.

Despite my uncle's cooperation, he was forced to sign the confession anyway. They declared that he was conspiring to cover up his relatives' subversive activities and issued threats on the lives of the entire family. The guards listed names and addresses and shared with him the order of the deaths, as they would occur, beginning with my grandparents. He had no choice but to sign. Instead of letting him go, they used his signed confession as evidence against him to convict him of crimes against the state, punishable by death. He was immediately scheduled for execution by firing squad. He was twenty years old.

The next morning, Tío Pedro was stripped down to his underwear and handcuffed. He was taken to a remote cell where he was left standing for a few minutes. Two officers guarded him as he faced a concrete wall. The stare of his executioners could have burned holes into his bare back. The awful silence was only broken by an occasional drill command from the officers outside, directing the troops in their morning exercises. Someone else stepped into the room, and a familiar voice halted the execution. Tío Pedro would later recognize the voice of Chilo, his distant cousin who happened to be a high-ranking police officer at the time. They returned my uncle to his cell but he was not released. He remained missing for over a month before my dad found him through the Red Cross. He had been detained in a subterranean jail for political prisoners not too far from our house.

My parents took turns visiting him for months and months. It was painfully obvious that the beatings never stopped. Nearly two years after his arrest, he was released under a Red Cross Amnesty Program, barely the shadow of a man.

Meanwhile we were taught to beware of the guerrilleros who swooped down from their mountain hideouts to snatch young children from their villages to fight a revolution they were too young to understand, much less truly believe in. Those "subversives" cheated their youngest fighters out of their childhoods, plucked them from the cotton fields, lured them from urban schools, taught them to bomb buses and blast roads apart, to leave innocent people stranded or dead in the name of the movement. They left their autograph behind on the walls of burnt-down buildings, the huge red letters proudly read: F.M.L.N., the handiwork of the Farabundo Marti Liberation Front. We were taught to despise even the graffiti, to ignore its presence, to look away.

Back in Santa Maria, six men, disheveled, dirty and heavily armed, stormed into my grandparents' home one night. They were guerrilleros, hiding from the National Guard. They demanded food and shelter from whatever home they invaded, without regard for the danger they dragged those families into. The gang took over their bedrooms, emptied their supply pantries, broke their clay pots, killed their chickens, and steeped the entire house with the stench of war. For eight days, they forced Mama Lidia to cook for them as they filled their bellies nonstop. Her worn hands were raw when they left at last. We were taught to hate those subversives. We could see first-hand their cruelty and disregard for order. It was easier to ignore the accounts of the many people who disappeared at the hands of the military when we had an evil subversive enemy so despised and feared.

When a boy who lived on our street received his first death threat, it all still seemed unreal. We called him "El Chino." He was eleven years old and full of energy. He played in every soccer match on the block and zigzagged through our neighborhood on his shiny banana-seat bike. He was accused of consorting with "subversives" even though he was just a child. Just a few days before the threat, he had come to my eleventh birthday party looking adorably awkward. His shiny black hair was combed and held in place with some concoction, surely of his own making. He wore the most neatly pressed outfit anyone had ever seen him wear. He handed me a present, about the size of the Lido cookie boxes that I loved receiving on my birthdays. He probably saved up for quite a while to get it for me. I offered him a sandwich, neatly wrapped in a printed-paper napkin and a cup of *horchata* from my tray. He ate cake and danced cumbias and Donna Summer tunes in our living room. He even took a swing at the last *piñata* ever hung in my honor. Later that week, "El Chino" disappeared. He was found shot through the neck on the passenger side of a car a few miles from his house. *Could this all be real?*

It was hard to ignore what was happening all around us. A classmate showed me a pamphlet about a massacre in a small town near the border with Honduras. Men, women, and children had been slaughtered all alike. I was never supposed to even look at this kind of stuff, but once I had, the graphic, bloody images were engraved in my mind. The brief paragraphs painted a gory picture of corpses and machine guns, severed limbs, and bayonets driven through babies' bodies. I gave the pamphlet back right away — I could not keep it for obvious reasons. Surely, a mindless hoax. Propaganda. Or could it be real?

Petty thieves used the war to their advantage too. After graduating from the Azcunaga School for Girls in 1980, Milady and I transferred to the private K-12 school across the street, where Sonia would complete her senior year and where we would enroll in the seventh grade. Sonia, Milady and I were together, with Daysi only a few steps away across the street. Tuition fees for the three of us were astronomical. My parents planned on transferring Daysi from the Azcunaga School for Girls when she completed the sixth grade in two years. The money was worth the pain. The private Liceo was considered much safer than public middle schools, which had become recruiting grounds for both sides of the war.

At a quarter to eight on a typical morning at my Liceo, students gathered in groups in the schoolyard, socializing before classes began. That morning, as every morning, my uniform was impeccable. My scooped-neck blouse was sparkling white; my mid-calf length olive skirt and vest bearing my school crest were meticulously pressed. The pleats on my skirt hardly moved as I walked across the concrete basketball court to meet my friends. The boys' plain olive pants and white button-down shirts were not quite as elaborate a uniform as the girls' were.

The basketball court took up the main part of the yard, with the back hoop resting against a tall, brick wall at the far end of campus. That basketball court served many purposes on our campus besides our short-lived basketball tournaments. With desks dragged out from the classrooms and neatly lined up, the court was the outdoor setting for the campus-wide midterms. Every eye squinted to read the exams as the white paper reflected the glare of the sun. The court was also the dance floor for the school's crowded end-of-year parties and it was the main thoroughfare for the students from the row of classrooms on the right side. The wide window frames of the classrooms had been left purposely without glass or drapes to allow ventilation. A small snack shop and three smaller classrooms enclosed the court on the left. Like most private K-12 schools, our Liceo offered only one classroom per grade. The rest of the rooms were to the left of the gate down a wide corridor.

The twelfth graders disappeared to their class down the hallway. They walked proud, tall, and unreachable: they were practically adults. They would complete their *bachillerato* by the end of the year. Some trained to be secretaries, others mechanics, and many of the more technical ones, like my sister Sonia, would receive degrees in accounting. The smallest number with academic majors would go on to the university. The seniors had earned their status. Their room at the west end of campus was so revered that the younger kids never set foot there. My sister Milady and I were in the same class, but she stood with her own group on the basketball court, a few feet away. We never spent time together unless we had to. We stood around casually in front of our teacher-less rooms, awaiting the bell that would start the day. It was a regular old morning.

Gunshots rang out, catching everyone mid-sentence and completely off guard. Bullets burst through our closed steel gates, sparking mayhem in the courtyard. Some children scattered while others dropped on the spot to take cover. Milady and I ran to hide in our classroom, too scared to drop down outside. The shrieks around the campus were as loud as the gunshots.

"What's happening?" I shouted.

"Just be quiet and wait," Milady ordered, as she crawled under a desk against the wall furthest from the door. I crawled under there with her and waited quietly. Other students from our class also came to hide. I did not know if Sonia had made it to campus from home yet that morning, since we never walked to school together from our home in Los Santos. Daysi was across the street at our old school for girls, so it was impossible to know that she was safe. The shots continued sporadically. I was terrified for my sisters.

I began whispering under my breath as many verses from Psalm 91 as I could remember; Mami had made us memorize it precisely for times like this.

"You will not fear the terror of night, nor the arrow that flies by day, nor the pestilence that stalks in the darkness, nor the plague that destroys at midday. A thousand may fall at your side, ten thousand at your right hand, but it will not come near you..."

Two more shots. I shut my eyes and held my arms tightly around my legs. My skirt dragged over my penny loafers onto the floor. I buried my face in my knees and the fabric of my uniform muffled my prayer. I needed to hear myself pray, so when I ran out of words, I repeated them time and time again. Minutes later, when only the echo of the gunfire remained, we heard the terrible shouting of a man whose voice we did not recognize, sounding loudly against our green walls.

The man shouting was a bus driver who had been robbed in front of our school. The robbers had forced him to block the street with the bus — a guerrilla trademark. However, petty thieves also used this tactic sometimes to discourage anyone from calling the authorities. Anyone with common sense would try to avoid becoming involved in a military conflict. The driver did as he was told, pointing the bus directly at our school gate. But after turning the bus, he refused to relinquish his cash box. Instead he panicked and ran, moneybox in hand, directly toward our school. His ticket taker, only a teenage boy, panicked as well, and ran after him. The robbers opened fire on them, hitting the driver several times in the back and wounding the boy in the head. A shower of bullets bypassed them both and burst through our school gate, hitting several people inside.

A second-grader was hit through the ankle as she ran. Our school principal was shot above the knee as he struggled to direct students to safety. The school custodian opened the punctured steel door to pull in the driver and the boy, who had both collapsed there. The robbers, still waiting to claim their loot, wanted to make sure the moneybox stayed where it was. They opened fire yet again: the last two shots. The custodian was hit in his right hip. One bullet shattered a few keys on the heavy ring hanging from his belt and lodged itself in his hipbone, shreds of keys and all. He plummeted to the ground with a loud thump. The thieves stopped their shooting spree after our kind janitor fell. They snatched the cash box from the bleeding driver, just inches from our school door, and fled.

After the gunfire ended, I looked outside. I crawled from under the desk and, against Milady's orders, I peeked out of my classroom's window. Teachers were dragging the driver, the boy, and our custodian away from the gate. Clumps of blood traced a ghastly path along the office hallway. An eighth-grade girl I did not know ran toward the office. She was sobbing with her hand over her mouth. Blinded by her own hysteria, she was completely unaware of what she would encounter. The driver reached up and grabbed her knee-length skirt as she rushed past him.

"Pray for me! I am dying..." he screamed.

She pulled away in horror, and collapsed into the arms of one of the helpless teachers, who surrounded the driver in his agony.

Sonia came to find Milady and me a few moments later. She forbid us to walk to the west end of campus, where the ticket boy was taken. His head wounds were so severe that he never had a chance. He was no more than fifteen years old. His dying words were for his mother. Although help was called right away, both the driver and the boy died in our schoolyard before the ambulance arrived nearly two hours later. The dozen or so injured survivors were taken to the hospital. The following week class was held as always, but the light shining through the holes in our school gate would not let us forget.

Examples of the military's ruthlessness surfaced later, like the massacre in the tiny village of El Mozote, in my mother's home state of Morazán. The town's people were humble, devoutly Christian, focused on working the fields. They struggled to live normal lives despite the war tearing apart the countryside around them and tried to stay out of the guerrilleros' path through town on their way into the mountains. A U.S.-trained battalion of the National Guard had a brief encounter with fleeing guerrillas near El Mozote. The town's single survivor described with vivid detail the morning the soldiers of the Atlacatl Battalion moved into the town. They interrogated the entire town for information about the guerrillas' identities, about their secret camps. But they knew nothing.

The Guards called everyone to the plaza, accused them of being "collaborators," and set out to execute the entire town. They butchered hundreds and hundreds of civilians. Many were shot, others stabbed, and some were locked into tiny huts and burned alive. Over three hundred of the victims were children under ten: at least fifty of them, only babies. Seventy-five of the victims were over sixty. Unable even to stand, a one-hundred-and-five-year-old man and his one-hundred-year-old companion had to be held up to be executed. Among the dead lay a sixteen-year-old paralyzed boy, a thirty-five-year old deaf-mute man, and about a dozen pregnant women. Farmers. Seamstresses. Bricklayers. Maguey spinners. Day laborers. Artisans. Entire families were wiped from existence. Some were even robbed of their names as they were murdered. The only trace left of the identity of many was a number and an estimated age on the sad list of seven hundred and sixty-seven exhumed victims, published later by the Archbishop's Office of Human Rights. Many other bodies not yet recovered may never be accounted for. It happened just one week after I had left the country with my family in 1981. It took over a decade for me to finally learn about it.

Many other hamlets suffered the fate of El Mozote. Many other atrocities took place too horrible to describe. At twelve years old, I was conditioned to ignore it all and keep silent. The National Guard was a constant presence, in a warped way, unseen and accepted as part of our culture. My parents had trained us well to stay out of trouble: Ask nothing, say nothing, do nothing. The rest of society and the media trained us to hate the subversives. We had to, to survive. I have since learned that no matter which side blamed which, innocent people were still murdered every day.

The echoes of the war reminded me of why we had to leave home. The image I held as a young child of a life in the United States was so different, so peaceful, and so perfect. Since we were very young, we had seen this different world through the eyes of my mother, who had worked there for many years. As our Guatemalan charter bus rode on, I knew a very different life awaited us on the other side.

LEMONS

"Here's your bread! Your quesadillas! Your semitas! Your menudencias!"

My mother started selling bread for the "Vicenta Bakery" when she was in the third grade. Her voice was as recognizable as the clanking of the oxen pulling carriages on the cobblestone streets of her hometown. Her constant smile was as familiar in the town of Chilanga as the summer rain. Every afternoon after school, she checked in with *Niña Chenta*, the town baker. She earned twenty-five cents for every forty pieces of *pan dulce* she sold. Niña Chenta filled a shallow basket with pastries of all kinds, and covered it with a large napkin. Mami left her notebooks behind the wooden counter and set off with her precious cargo propped on her shoulder. Folks strolled out of their doorways like clockwork to buy her sweet cakes and biscuits.

"Here's your bread! Your *marquesotes*! Your *biscotelas*! *Your quesadillas!*", she shouted, loudly enough to be heard over the roar of the mills crushing corn into *masa.*

The gingham patterns on her snug dresses were bleached away by the sun. The fragile fabric right above the waist, scrubbed the hardest when washed, had been worn away by countless washes in the river. Her knee-length *manta* aprons were gathered at the waistline and switched back and forth as she walked. Mami's fair skin tanned easily under the afternoon sun. She often balanced the basket on her head to shelter her face and to rest her arm for a while. She pulled her thick black hair back in a long swinging ponytail to get it out of the way. Her bare feet, not used to the comfort of shoes, had grown accustomed to the sharp pebbles on the road as she set out on her daily quest.

Mami often walked out of her normal route just to sell an extra piece of bread so she could earn her full commission. Twenty-five cents in those days could buy a meal for the family, vegetables to make soup, a few tortillas and chicharrones, or bananas for everyone at home. When she did not sell enough, Niña Chenta paid her with a piece of *pan dulce*. Sometimes, she gobbled it all up, exhausted from her afternoon trek. But the image of her younger brothers never left her. When she started working for the bakery, Carlos was seven, Hildo was five, and German was two. The guilt often made her bring the tiny morsel home to share with them. The number of awaiting siblings grew and grew over time, but Niña Chenta's rewards stayed the same.

By her early teens, Mami was buying, selling, trading, sharing, marketing, manufacturing, and investing, all to help her parents support her six younger brothers and sisters... The tiny town of Chilanga had never seen a more promising young entrepreneur. She set up vending booths for fruit punch, cookies, coconut candy, and cigarettes. Town fairs and Sunday soccer games gave way to her shaved ice empire: her concession stands complete with homemade strawberry and pineapple syrups were a hit. She helped my grandmother, Mama Lola, buy and sell all kinds of fruits, cheese, sardines, lemons, and dried shrimp at the marketplace in the nearest town, over three kilometers away. They often trekked on the shade less road to San Francisco Gotera, with baskets full of goods early in the morning. Both of their dresses had the familiar worn-out spot over their bellies. Cotton towels twisted into *yaguales* cushioned the load on their heads. Mami's lustrous hair and Mama Lola's beautiful curls were neatly braided. Mami took two steps for every one of Mama Lola's. Their feet had to move quickly across the searing earth to avoid being burnt. She dreamed of getting her own pair of high-heeled shoes one day, so she would not have to borrow her neighbors' to go to the weekend dances in the Plaza. My mother was well into her teens before owning her first pair of shoes.

There were two main family businesses. My grandfather Jeronimo, Papa Chombo, worked in construction and Mama Lola was a seamstress. Without much access to ready-made clothes in town, Mama Lola's business was steady, but hardly enough to make ends meet. Money was extremely tight during the six months of rain every year, when Papa Chombo could not build houses.

The old-fashioned wrought iron sewing machine was the family's most prized possession. Mami loved to rock her baby brothers and sisters to sleep on the full-sized pedal. Mami loved to clean the machine. She oiled it and shined it whenever she had the chance. Over the years, Mama Lola taught Mami to make paper wreaths for *El Dia de Los Muertos* in November, and taffeta rose buds for Mother's Day, red for mothers who were living, white for mothers who were not. One day, Mami took some leftover fabric and thread, and convinced Mama Lola to let her make some rag dolls to sell. A few hours later, Mami had finished making half a dozen of the ugliest dolls ever made. But she set out anyway, determined to come back with money for dinner. If she could not sell them, she would try to make *trueques,* or trades for food or other valuables. She hit the jackpot when she came across a little girl and her mother on their way back into town.

The lady was carrying a cage with three full-grown chickens in one hand, and a bag full of groceries in the other. Her little girl threw a tantrum, she cried and begged her mother to buy one of Mami's dolls. The little brat whined and shouted as though her life depended on taking Mami's doll home but the helpless lady had spent all her money at the market. Mami proposed an exchange that would normally sound crazy. But in the hysteria of her daughter's tantrum and the weight of her groceries and her own impatience, the poor lady could not refuse it. Mami smiled and rushed home with one less doll and a precious chicken flapping its wings under her arm.

Mami could no longer study once she went to work and sell full-time. She had a seventh grade education and a reputation as the savviest kid around. Don Osiel, an influential family friend, recommended Mami to teach for the Rural Literacy Program. This change sent her away from the path of harsh physical labor most others in town were destined for. Papa Chombo died the day after Mami's twentieth birthday. Mami's youngest brother, Tío Salomon, was only six years old.

After his death, Mami helped Mama Lola gather enough money to build a home. It was a white adobe house facing the corner of Chilanga's first major intersection, the first tangible accomplishment of which Mami could be proud.

• • •

Not far away, a little boy was growing up into the man that would become my father. He was the fourth oldest of nine children, raised in Santa Maria, a small town about an hour north of the Pacific Coast.

Each morning at his house, light fought its way in through the crevices around the thick wooden windows, which stayed shut all night with heavy latches. Once the windows were opened, light streamed in, reflecting off the dust particles rising from the floor. Thick *petates* stood neatly rolled up, leaning against the corners of the large room. The crunchy straw mats softened only after being slept on a few hundred times. Sunrise found the entire house up and ready for the day's work: school for the young ones, the cotton fields for the rest. The aroma of coffee brewed with cinnamon sticks weaved its way through the house long after everyone had gone.

"¡*Bajáte ya, Juan, que ya no caben!*", my father heard Mama Lidia shout.

Perched high on a branch of the calabash tree, Papi threw the last *jícara* down to his mother below. She managed to stretch the *matate* enough to squeeze in one more. He carried the string bag replete with *jícara*s, large and small, for Mama Lidia to make her flawless *guacales*. Once home, she carefully split them open, scraped them clean, and dried them in the sun. She made gourds like this to sell for a penny a piece at the marketplace in town.

In the adobe kitchen, she used her *guacales* for everything: from scoops, to cooking utensils, to large shiny bowls. After everyone left for the fields, Mama Lidia fed the chickens and tended to the rose bushes surrounding her shrine to the Virgin Mary out back, close to the water well. From the porch, she picked up one of the huge baskets she used to carry fruit into the town market the day before. She placed it in a corner on the kitchen's packed dirt floor, stacked with the other baskets she used to sell her fruit. She poured herself some water to drink from a large clay jug into one of her small homemade *guacales* and began preparing for everyone's return from the fields. She fried yucca and plantains, made tortillas, rice and beans, and sometimes, white bean soup with pigs' feet. In their rare times of plenty, the family feasted with her beef soup, shrimp, or *carne asada* for dinner. Evenings ended early at my father's house as everyone turned in to be up at dawn the next day to do it all again.

As the rest of the house caught their last few moments of sleep, a candle flickered on the wall of the living room and on my father's notebook. His homework had to be finished before sunrise each morning. During every school vacation, Papi reported to the fields with his brothers and Papa Chepe. The "kid" crew assisted the adults, fetching things for them and removing weeds from the endless rows of crops.

Sometimes they let the children work in groups of three to do the work of one adult. They were given a *tarea*, the task for the day, normally to harvest three rows of cotton, coffee, or corn, each a quarter mile long. This would normally take from early morning to early dusk. After finishing only the sixth grade, Papi left school to go to work in the fields as an "adult".

Like his own father and older brothers before him, he hoisted the filled sacks upon his back day in and day out. The harsh hours of picking sculpted my father's muscles over the years. The fields bronzed every bit of skin left uncovered. He inherited the rest of his looks from his maternal grandmother, Joaquina, the town's candle maker: her full lips, her wavy black hair, her Mayan nose, and her dark brown eyes deeper than a moonless night.

At eighteen, he worked as a bookkeeper for a local Hacienda. He sat up tall at the table in the office, carefully adding, subtracting, multiplying, and dividing right onto the boss's payroll ledgers, using nothing but a pencil and his mind. Any mistake meant either shortchanging a worker or losing his job for overpaying. He often stayed late double-checking his numbers on the ledger by candlelight to make sure they were right. He was nineteen before he tore himself from the fields to go to work at a factory in San Salvador.

My father worked in the printing department of the IUSA textile factory. He was devoted to finishing his high school degree through night classes. He eventually became fascinated with algebra... later he held weekend math competitions for my sisters and me. He eagerly hosted our matches right on the dining room table. My father worked religiously in his factory days, as always, every morning up at dawn, never back before twilight. I rarely meet people with a stronger work ethic than my father's.

My mother got a job as a laboratory technician at my father's factory, where they met in the mid-1960s. They were soon married and my sisters and I were born.

Our first home was the small two-bedroom apartment my parents bought in 1969, the year I was born, where I lived with my mom, dad and my three sisters. It was on the second floor of a six-story building, part of a large urban housing development in West San Salvador. Today, there is no trace left of our life there. Not a puff of smoke from Papi's cigarettes, nor the glow from our tiny metallic silver Christmas tree, not a leftover cumbia from our birthday parties or the pitter-patter of our feet against the polished concrete floors. Not even the bright pink paint on the concrete block walls remains.

Our apartment was only a short walk from the local K-12 school, past the neighborhood's cul-de-sac, across the huge soccer field. The bleachers that overflowed at every Sunday match with the neighbors' cheers were empty as we crossed that field each day struggling to save our freshly shined shoes from the dust cloud rising around us.

Our apartment building sat only yards from a dense ravine. We never really got too close, but we knew there were many people living there, in *champitas*, or shacks on the hillside. Once in a while, my father and I walked to my pediatrician's office in the wealthier part of town. The office was a thirty-minute bus ride away or just a mile's walk on a steep, packed-dirt road climbing out of the ravine next to our complex. Dad always chose the shorter route when he took me to the doctor after work. He held my hand so I would keep up with his long strides. My father's hand was three times the size of mine, always warm and gentle, even as he tugged me along when I slowed down to look at how different life was, just a few steps away from us.

The distinct smell of wet earth and a thick canopy of trees unmistakably marked our path. The road was a stairway, with large corrugated pipes and tree roots embedded across it all the way up. The hands of the *tortilleras* clapped away all around us, preparing dinnertime orders. We were surrounded by the buzz of chatter and gossip of the neighborhood's wives, sisters, and daughters who walked long and far to buy the freshest tortillas. The road took us past rows and rows of makeshift homes with walls and roofs molded out of cardboard and large banana tree leaves. The luckier ones had metal sheets to protect them from the rain. Scrawny dogs, with ribs showing through their dirty fur, crossed our path scavenging for food. The champas were so buried in the sloping foliage that it was difficult to spot them unless you walked right past them. There were many small children, with ragged clothes and bulging bellies, and huge bright eyes. The *Acelhuate River* running at the gorge's bottom was more than likely their drinking water and sewage system in one. I remember playing softball with some of these children many times, noticing their dusty bare feet without realizing the terrible poverty that they represented. We played countless games on our make-believe softball diamond, where we ran and laughed and won and lost all the same.

The children of the *champitas* never enjoyed the holidays quite as much as I did. At Christmas and New Year's Eve, my sisters and I roamed our suburban streets unsupervised, in sparkling, brand new clothes. We circled the neighborhood following the sounds of Olivia Newton-John, Leo Dan, ABBA, Hermanos Flores, and Earth Wind and Fire that spilled out of open doorways and weaved their way through the streets. We chased the aroma of *pupusas* from the corner stands that masked the smell of our burnt firecrackers.

In the small towns where my grandparents lived, Easter processions rivaled Christmas in their grandeur. The entire town marched to the beat of a hometown band: the women bowed their lace-covered heads, the men held their beaten straw hats across their chests. They hummed unfamiliar hymns along stone-covered streets with the children following closely behind. Saints' images and statuettes lavished with decorations were carried with stilts above the crowd. Churches and homes alike were decorated with brilliantly colored paper flowers, like the ones Dad's own mother crafted every year. Even the cemeteries bore the bright decorations that never wilted come morning... the spirits of heaven were celebrated with as much devotion and cheer as life itself.

The house my parents bought when I was ten was a dream come true. The smell of wet cement from the buildings still under construction, and of the freshly cut banana trees from the shrinking fields around us, lingered in our home. We watched the town grow over a short time. Our porch changed looks a few times, and the neighbors added to their small homes, but some details never changed. No matter how much time passed, the small store at the house around the corner, which opened shortly after we moved there, was always known as the "New Store." Every afternoon around the same time, a group of boys from down the block zigzagged past our main street on their glittery bikes with multi-colored fringes on the handles flapping every which way. Soccer matches were played like clockwork on the average weekend somewhere in the neighborhood. The first week we moved in, we heard a vendor lady walking tirelessly up and down our street. She carefully balanced a huge basket of vegetables and meats on top of her head. She still chanted as loudly as ever to sell her goods the week that we left.

Early on, however, my parents decided that one of them should move to the U.S. to work, only for a few months, to save money and help create a better future for the family. It was clear to them both that, no matter what, the family would never move away from El Salvador. They would not risk 'losing' the values they held so dear. They were convinced that all children in the U.S. are rebellious and disrespectful of their parents. In the U.S., they rationalized, children demand too much freedom, and they even have sex before marriage! Birth control pills are so common over there, that some parents even buy them for their own daughters! The thought alone was appalling. I can hear their absolute conclusion as if I had been there.

"No, no, and no. We will never move."

Only one of them would go, work for a while, and return just as soon as possible. That was the only way. Many factors had to be considered before deciding which one of them should do it. Their only connection to the U.S. was Bertha, one of my mother's mentors and good friend living in Washington D.C. Mami had a distinctly better disposition toward change, she always had. Dad had a higher salary at the factory, and more seniority toward his pension. Most importantly, they felt that a household with four young daughters would be more respected by others if a man headed it. So the choice was made and my mom made plans to leave as soon as they could scrape enough money for the trip. It was 1973 and I was not quite four years old.

FAREWELLS

Just before my mother's twenty-seventh birthday, my parents took my sisters and me to a park where my dad would take some photos of us. Mami dressed each of us in matching white cotton blouses with ruffled sleeves and bright red apple appliqués on the front pocket. She wore her hair down and the dangling gold earrings she only wore on special occasions. Mami wanted to pose with each one of us leaning in to kiss her cheek. Her sadness was obvious even to me, at four years old but I did not realize why. A few days later, she would depart for the United States for the first time, leaving her husband, her four daughters, her job, and her entire life behind.

The reason for Mami's leaving was impossible for my parents to explain and even more impossible for the four of us to understand. It took me over twenty years to finally learn the details of each of her three trips to the United States. My mother had sporadically shared these details with us over the years. Without fail, these stories made my sisters and I think,

"Oh boy, heeeeere we go again..."

Our mental whining always distracted us just long enough to miss the point.

Mami made her first trip with Carmen, the sister of her friend Bertha. My parents pulled every string known to them to get Mami's temporary visa. It was only good for two weeks, but it was good enough to get her out of the country. They would fly to Los Angeles and then to Virginia, where Bertha lived. This was

Mami's first time in an airplane. She was so nervous that she did not have time yet to miss us. No one should suspect that they planned to overstay their visas, but they wanted to avoid any sort of questioning that might point out their nervousness. They reached the Los Angeles International Airport six hours later. Naturally, the U.S. customs process was a lot more thorough than the exit process out of San Salvador. The wait was long but eventually they went through without incident.

They trekked across the LAX facility, temporary visas in hand, to the United domestic flight terminal. They only had two carry-on bags each but they started to weigh more with each step. Carmen sat down on an indoor bench, across from the ticket purchasing line, while Mami stood in line to check in. It seemed that the whole world had decided to travel to Virginia that evening, taking along every piece of luggage they owned. Mami stared impatiently at the linoleum floor, trying desperately not to stand out. She asked for help in Spanish, and one of the clerks walked over to assist her. The clerk printed their tickets and asked to speak to Carmen. Mami signaled to her from the counter, and Carmen reluctantly walked over. She looked at the passport photo to confirm her identity and smiled at her. The clerk pointed them toward the gate for their flight to Dulles International, where Bertha would await them. They walked away without looking back.

The hours in the air were simply endless; they camouflaged themselves among the passengers by intently "reading" the English in-flight magazines from cover to cover. The clerk had forgotten to tell them about the flight's two layovers. Each flight was short enough not to have meal service. They ate nothing but peanuts for twelve hours. Each time they landed, Mami gathered her few things and quietly asked the flight attendant, "Washington?" To Mami's dismay, each time she heard "No." Thankfully, Carmen and Mami got away without having to change planes or find their way through English-only terminals. Their plane reached Virginia early the next morning, and not a moment too soon. Exhausted from their long journey and terrified of being questioned by airport security, they locked themselves up in a bathroom stall at the terminal. They had told Bertha where to look for them. Over two hours later, Bertha found them huddled, worried and starving. She rushed them to the car to take them to their new home.

After barely enough time to get over her jet lag, Mami began her first job as a live-in housekeeper, two days later. When she was asked if she had a Visa or work permit, she answered "yes" but they did not require her to produce proof. Mami spoke no English. She began work right away, communicating with hand signals and by pointing her way around the house. Bertha helped her as an over-the-phone translator for more complex tasks. Mami cleaned the house and looked after the three young girls in the family. The oldest girl was nine and the middle one was five. Mami spent most of her day with the little one, who was a toddler just about Daysi's age then. For her work, she earned twelve dollars a day, most of which she sent to us in El Salvador.

Mami kept herself busy all the time, even in her basement bedroom at night. She bought an English textbook to teach herself at night. She stayed up even later whenever she gave herself the tests in her book. With her hair rolled into a shiny bun, she sat on the twin bed with the book across her lap. She huddled close to the nightstand to harness the brightness of the small lamp on the pages, much like my dad had done as a boy by candlelight. She practiced her pronunciation on her own, never quite sure if it was correct, writing each word first then forcing herself to read it out loud. For hours, she scribbled and recited. Scribble, recite. Scribble, recite.

I wash the clothes: "I gwash deh cloats."

She goes to school: "Chee gos to eskool."

Johnny wants to drive: "Yony gwans to dribe."

The walls of her tiny room seemed to close in on her. She purposely left the lamp on most nights. She let the glow reflect off the window-less walls, hoping the light might keep them from caving in as she slept. Within three months, her late study nights began to pay off. Her vocabulary grew and her pronunciation got better. Soon she was able to function more and more without Bertha's help.

She also wrote to us constantly, often on special stationery she bought from the nearby drugstore. She used note cards with cute animal babies, pretty birds, flowers, and butterflies, or "Holly Hobby" characters. When we received her cards and letters, I secretly compared mine with my sisters'. I fell in love with whichever card had my name, convinced Mami had picked the prettiest one just for me. She thought about us constantly. Only the memories of us could warm her heart through that first bitter winter, alone in the U.S.

One job was never enough. Mami took odd jobs whenever she could, waiting tables one week or cleaning offices on evenings another... all to make extra money for us. On weekends, she worked at a cafeteria on the George Washington University campus. There were hundreds of other kitchen workers there, clad in hairnets and different color uniforms to distinguish themselves among the different crews. The daily hustle and bustle left little time for much else, but in 1974, Mami stumbled onto the Hispanic Catholic Center in Maryland. She enrolled in their GED program and after many nights of hard work, she received her High School Diploma in September 1975. The family was overcome with joy. We celebrated Mami's triumphant moment together, in our hearts and minds.

Her stay in Washington D.C. had a short interruption. Weary and homesick beyond words, she returned home for Christmas that year, but neither my sisters nor I have any recollection of her brief visit.

I was six years old.

Still with the dream of a better life in mind, Mami headed back to Washington in January of 1976. This time she traveled alone, flying with a tourist visa to Miami International Airport. An INS officer stopped her before she could make the transfer to her Washington flight. When the officer questioned her about her final destination, she maintained that she was only in Florida as a tourist. The officer searched her seeking proof that she intended to overstay her visa and found a phone number with no area code in her purse. It was Bertha's number in D.C. He rushed to the Immigration office right in the airport terminal, with Mami in his custody, to research the number locally. Of course, they were unsuccessful. They had no clue that she had numerous letters to be delivered in Washington, the plane tickets for her next flight, and her United States address book tucked away in other compartments of her purse. As she sat outside a cubicle office waiting for the officers, she placed her coat over the purse and put every incriminating document into the lining of her coat sleeve. She had ripped the sleeve at the inside seam to hide away money during the trip. Her coat was never searched. They had no choice but to release her. She exchanged her expired ticket for a new flight to Washington and returned to work at the GW cafeteria.

Just two short months later, on the only day Mami had been bed-ridden sick in years, there was an INS raid at the university kitchen. Everyone apprehended was ordered to leave the country within two months. She could not simply show up for work the next day. After discussing the close call over the telephone with my dad, they decided to have her immediately begin looking into jobs at the homes of diplomats in the area, where she might be sheltered from danger.

Soon after that, a Brazilian friend of Mami's from the Catholic Center pointed her in the right direction. Mami was hired one month later as the personal assistant to the wife of the Brazilian Ambassador to the U.S. Ten other employees completed the staff of the diplomat's home: a chef and two helpers, a butler, two gardeners, and four maids. As the lady's personal assistant, Mami's job involved meticulous work. Mami was paid to take care of every tiny detail, to look after her employer's every whim, to endure her every tantrum.

"Rosario, I want my blue suit for tomorrow with the white silk blouse and my white pumps. And my pink scarf. Pressed."

"Rosario, I thought I mentioned I don't like my toast crunchy. Is that too difficult to remember?"

"Rosario, this toothpaste tastes different. You wouldn't buy a different brand without checking with me first, would you?"

The air in this home was heavy with the formality of a true bureaucracy, down to the servants-only elevator and back entrance and the servants' mandatory change of clothes. The ritual included the switching of uniforms before supper, from daytime green to evening black. Her black mid-calf dress came with matching white apron and hat. After preparing the beds and laying out the lady's nightgown, she retired to her small bedroom on the fourth floor along with the other servants.

The U.S. Bicentennial fireworks lit up the sky over Washington D.C. and the Massachusetts Avenue embassy. Mami got a peek of the show through the sliding bedroom window, after a full day's work. Many of the capital's landmarks were within reach, but she seldom had the time or the freedom to go enjoy them.

She often squeezed her way past the twin mattress and leaned against the windowsill, with the drapes pulled and the bare light bulb overhead turned off. The starry night sky hypnotized her. She knew those very stars also watched over her daughters so far away. The demands of the job exceeded even my mother's threshold for pain.

In 1977, Mami went to work as a babysitter for a Georgetown family on N Street. She joined a staff of three others. She stayed in a wide corner room across from the elevator on the second floor. The home's third-floor penthouse had a sunroom with a gorgeous view of the Potomac River. Mami seldom visited the sunroom except when serving tea for the lady and her guests. Mami's days started early and ended late. She cleaned and assisted the chef with the nightly formal dinner affairs, serving the warmed china plates and removing them only two at a time. She served after-dinner coffee and turned down the beds each night. My mother was at their beck and call, summoned by the service bell at anytime. She also looked after the family's two young children, a boy and a girl. She remained there nearly a year.

Mami came to life in the letters and photographs she sent every chance she got... We received a picture of Mami in a white uniform giving a birthday gift to the little Georgetown girl whom she looked after. The girl's reddish freckles, blonde Shirley-Temple curls, and bluest of eyes reminded me of the beautiful dolls Mami always sent us. I couldn't have hated that little girl more if I had tried. I held the picture trying to imagine myself in her place, receiving the coveted present from my mother's hands... But I simply could not see myself in her. My eyes hadn't the slightest trace of blue. My thick hair was too black. My brown skin was too dark. *Morena. Negra. Negrita.* The nicknames my family had given me with love were painful reminders of the type of "beauty" I could never have, the "beauty" I admired and resented all at once. Blinded by envy, my eyes simply could not see my own gifts. The mirror revealed something that could never live up to the foreign ideal of my dolls or the little Georgetown girl. I hated her for having Mami instead of us. Thankfully, Mami returned to us in early 1978 to be home for my imminent eye operation. I was in the fourth grade.

My sisters and I were ecstatic to have her back. I was terrified of the hospital, but in a way I knew that were it not for that, Mami might not have come home that year. Her arrival was truly special. We had special permission from the principal to leave school early that day. Our classmates and friends were as excited for us as we were for ourselves. Like most people we knew, they wished constantly to be connected to the United States somehow. The connection could be a worthless gift, a leftover pencil or notebook, maybe even a toy. Whatever it was, it would serve as a bragging piece for a good few weeks.

Any one of our friends would have loved to trade places with us, but we were the lucky ones. After picking Mami up from the airport, we spent a few days at home, sorting through the goodies. The boxes of gifts she brought had a distinct scent which my sisters and I learned to recognize as the United States itself. We picked out clothes and toys when we were given the choice. We admired the gadgets she brought for the kitchen, which we could not touch nor comprehend. A few weeks later when my surgery date neared, I was taken to the hospital for the first hospital stay of my life. I do not remember much about my stay at Children's Hospital, except for the ridiculously long lines and for the fact that my mother was there with me.

After my operation, Mami was supposed to stay home for good. Her fluency in English and her early teaching experience in her hometown placed her as an English instructor at a private school in San Salvador. In 1979, my parents bought a two-bedroom house in a new housing development in the suburban town of Soyapango, *Reparto Los Santos.* Much of the neighborhood was still under construction when we moved in. Many houses were still missing their rooftops at the time. The grooved sections of Duralita were installed at a slant to route the rain to one side of the house. We waited over two months before our water and electricity services were hooked up. As we watched the neighborhood of Los Santos grow, our yellow house changed too. My parents built a large bedroom for my sisters and me, with a open water reservoir out back, on what used to be our back yard. The water basin was critical since we could never quite depend on our local water supply. Our sloped front yard became a shady, concrete porch enclosed by a striped yellow canopy. Our dream of a "better" life was fast becoming a reality, but it all came at a cost.

In June of 1980, my family's financial picture was quickly deteriorating. Mami reluctantly returned to work in the U.S. This time she traveled to Los Angeles with my father's sister-in-law, Isabel. They were equipped only with four hundred dollars each and my mother's experience. They traveled through Mexico by bus and train with no visas and no paid guides, or *coyotes*. They had to save half of their money for the border crossing alone. Once reaching Tijuana, Mami exchanged the high heels she had worn since El Salvador for some leather sandals to make the trek across the border more bearable. She seldom wore anything but high heels; they helped bump her just over her five-foot frame. Mami's well-defined calves, the result of years of working on her feet, would need to toil even harder on their trip to the other side.

Mami and Isabel were dropped off at an abandoned building in San Luis Río Colorado. They were with a coyote, and a few other people, including two small children. The guarded border gate was visible just east of their hiding place. The wire fence separating the two countries stood about fifty yards in front of them. The coyote pointed out the hole in the ground beneath the fence directly across from them. They would be crawling through it to get across. He also pointed out the road that stretched along the U.S. side, parallel to the border. Beyond the road, endless lemon fields would provide excellent cover for them even under the blazing noontime sun.

An INS truck diligently patrolled the road. Once the truck disappeared into the summer heat rising from the asphalt, the coyote signaled. The group sprinted across the fifty-yard stretch and rushed one by one through the hole below the fence to the other side. They piled up on the flat bed of a pickup truck, which pulled up just as they reached the road. The truck took them into the lemon fields where they hid under the trees for many hours. The group was left behind with very little water and food. Even the shade of the lemon trees lost its coolness beneath the fierce desert sun. When the water in the plastic jugs ran out, they pulled lemons off the trees to suck on for moisture. Mami gathered up the garbage to give to the coyote when he returned, to leave no trace of their presence. They waited there, surrounded in crusty peels, hungry, tired, and parched well into the night. The sour taste remained on their palates for days.

When the truck returned just past midnight, the coyote rushed everyone onto the back of the truck. He told everyone to lie down head-to-toe. He covered the crowded platform with a few flimsy wooden boards to support a full load of used car tires. The old tires were stacked eight or nine high, tied down and held together with old dirty ropes. He left but a few small openings for ventilation through the foul-smelling rubber. And thus they rode, concealed in their dark and unbearably cramped hiding space, on the verge of suffocation, all except Mami. She was an asset to the coyote: she was assertive, bilingual, and quick to think on her feet. She rode in the passenger seat with the driver all the way to Los Angeles, where they arrived the next morning. Mami and Isabel were dropped off by the coyote at Tío German's studio apartment near Western and Seventh Street, in the not-so-glamorous heart of Los Angeles. The cycle would begin again.

Mami started working immediately. She was hired as a nanny and housekeeper for a wealthy family in the west side, referred by a friend of a friend. Her ease with the language and comforting smile made her interview go smoothly.

"Have you ever taken care of children before?"

"Oh, yes, I work with children many years. Since nineteen...seventy-three. I work with many families in Washington – Georgetown."

"What ages were the children?"

"From babies to ten years old," Mami replied, "And I have four daughters too, from nine to fifteen years."

"Where are your daughters now?"

"In El Salvador."

"Are you married?"

"Yes, my husband stays in El Salvador with my daughters."

"How long have you been in Los Angeles?"

"One month."

"I would like to talk to your last employer in Washington."

Mami's smile didn't waver.

"Well, I am sure we can find the telephone number but I don't have it anymore. They are called the Johnsons."

They talked about her years at the Johnson's in Georgetown. There was no reference to visas or anything of the sort. She was hired.

Mami looked after the couple's young boy and cleaned the four-bedroom house. She worked twelve-hour days most days, never earning more than $25 dollars per day. She spent weekends at the one-bedroom apartment with Tío German, along with his wife Tita, his sister-in-law Daisy, and Mami's sister

Melba. After exhausting weeks at their respective jobs, they crashed on the living room carpet of the tiny place, crowding the floor with pillows and blankets every Friday and Saturday night. On occasion, none of them would work extra days and the weekend would bring a bit of welcome rest, but that was not always the case. The dreaded feeling of Monday seemed to hang around the tiny apartment all week long. Each of their exhausted faces told the story of their own odyssey and sacrifice for the families they left thousands of miles away.

Fourth of July, 1980. In Los Angeles, a few days before July Fourth, as the city prepared for the patriotic festivities, Mami prepared for her first day off since she arrived. She had planned to go bargain shopping for her first package home; she even had the bus routes planned out, holiday schedules and all. But her employer would not let her off that day. She told Mami that it was Independence Day for the U.S., not for her. A slap in the face would sting less. She quit that housekeeping job within days. She left there and took a job at an outdoor equipment manufacturer where she worked until the following spring.

That same July weekend, we received news of a deadly trip involving about thirty Salvadorans. I was ten years old when the news hit the headlines in San Salvador. Hoping to start a new life in the United States, the group set out bound for Los Angeles. Instead, they were robbed and abandoned by coyotes in the Arizona desert, with no food or water. Thirteen of the immigrants died: ten of them were women as young as thirteen years old. Countless newspapers published headlines and pictures about their terrible ordeal in the Organ Pipe Cactus National Park. We heard about these unfortunate folks being forced to drink any liquid available to them to stay alive... cologne, aftershave lotion, even sweat and urine. I felt a distinct connection to these people.

Like my own mother one month before, they began their trek to the U.S. with nothing but hopes for a better future. The headline of the Los Angeles Times front page on Monday, July 7, 1980 echoed the tragic reports in newspapers back home.

"ALIENS LEFT TO DIE IN DESERT."

I looked at the photos of the stranded travelers, their faces were scarred by pain and broken hopes. Their tired eyes, young and old alike, reflected the tragic images of their loved ones who died before them. These people could have been my relatives, my neighbors, my teachers, my friends. There was nothing remotely "alien" about any of them. When the papers brought news of these people at age ten, I wept. I was terrified by the concept of my own mother possibly being trapped in such a deadly situation. When I think about these people today, I gasp, frozen by the mere idea of struggling to survive in their scorched shoes. I know that my fate and my family's might have been the same if things had not worked out as well as they did.

•   •   •

Our expectations and dreams were formed slowly over the years. Our indirect yet constant exposure to the United States was uncommon in our neighborhoods and schools. Our classmates revered our "American" connection. My sisters and I had plenty of opportunity to develop a clear image of The United States, an image as perfect as it was naive. Throughout her years in the U.S., Mami had worked at countless fast food restaurants, factories, and stores to make extra money for us. We focused on the perfect promise of America, not on the harsh physical labor Mom endured to buy every frilly dress and fancy toy. I lived many fantasies through the photos and letters she sent us over the years, which we cherished more than life itself.

I imagined myself strolling down the clean, tree-lined streets of her Maryland neighborhood. I wondered how it would feel to order food from a car through a clown's head, like Mami's picture at a drive-through restaurant in Washington. Driving through anywhere, especially restaurants, was a concept unknown in our country. I yearned to play in the snow someday and wear heavy wool coats, like Mami did through her winters in Virginia. I saw myself attending her graduation in 1975, hearing her name, and watching her stroll onto the stage, smiling with her head lifted high. How I wished to see first hand the smile on her graduation portrait and feel firsthand the joy we could not share in person... I fantasized about splashing around in the gated swimming pool of her apartment building, in the place she called "the Valley."

When I was about eight years old, before we ever studied it in school, my sisters and I wished to speak

English so much that we invented a game called "translation." We held conversations speaking our own version of "English," mumbling and rambling, pausing to write down its meaning in Spanish, and later reading the nonsense to each other. We owe many afternoon laughs to our silly game. Our wish to be bilingual had started to come true when Mami began teaching us the language at home before her last trip to the U.S.

Most of all, I fantasized about the six of us being together again. I dreamt about the cab rides through the long, lit tunnel near the airport when we went there to pick her up. I thought about peering through the tall terminal windows at the crowds emerging from each plane onto the wheeled stairwells. I closed my eyes when I blew out the candles on the many birthday cakes we cut in Mami's absence, wishing to open my eyes and see her standing at the door.

•   •   •

Mami returned to El Salvador the day before my twelfth birthday, in 1981. Two years into the civil war, the political situation in El Salvador was likely to get much worse before it got any better. This time she returned to El Salvador to bring our whole family to the U.S. with her. Although I was very young, in a way, I had been preparing for this move my entire life.

We did not have Visas to enter the United States, but my parents were determined on the move. Mom and Dad filed for tourist Visas for Mexico City. They were slightly easier to receive, although still considered a luxury. In order to receive tourist Visas to another country, especially the U.S., my parents first had to prove to the Salvadoran Embassy that they had every intention of returning. The government needed tangible proof: property deeds, bank statements, investment documents. But like most people in El Salvador, we had none of those things. We had to manage without U.S. visas. My parents called in every favor and talked to every inside connection they had at the embassy or at any official office, but they were still only able to get us restricted tourist permits to the immediate Mexico City area. These would be good enough to get us out of the country.

The trips for the five of us would set my family back nearly four thousand dollars. The bus and train trip through Mexico cost two thousand, and the trip from Mexicali to the U.S. alone cost another two. Fifty percent of this of this hefty fee had to be paid up front; the other fifty percent would be paid upon our safe arrival at my relatives' apartment in the Pico Union District of Downtown L.A. My father would remain behind and wait until the rest of his retirement funds were available before starting his own trip.

And so it was decided that we must travel without him.

•   •   •

The bus ride through Guatemala was long, uneventful, and boring.

My sisters and I spoke very little during this part of the trip. At dawn of Day Two, we reached the Mexican border. Mami led us stumbling out, half asleep to trade buses again, found seats in the same exact arrangement, and rode on. The sky was a deep fluorescent navy. A gorgeous sunrise was imminent but I could not stay awake to witness it. When I awoke later that morning, we were pulling off the road to a restaurant shaped like a big straw hut. This breakfast was my first encounter with authentic Mexican food. After inhaling our meal of *huevos rancheros*, ultra-thin hand made tortillas and fresh-squeezed orange juice, we reboarded and continued our treacherous ride, which tortured our rear ends without mercy.

We reached Mexico City close to eight in the evening of December eleventh, the brink of the City's foremost religious holiday, the day of the *Virgen de Guadalupe*. Mami wanted us to experience the festivities. We put our few bags into lockers at the bus station and began our walk to the Basilica of Guadalupe, the main church where the celebration takes place. At Mami's request, Sonia's new friend, Víctor, and the two other young men who were traveling with him joined us in our evening stroll. A woman traveling with her four daughters was a conspicuous sight, so she felt slightly safer with this arrangement. They appeared to be decent people. She insisted that the streets would soon be flooded with people celebrating, but I knew better. After all, it was so late.

As I walked next to my little sister in the chilly evening air, our breath froze before our eyes for the first time in our lives. I was extremely excited! Until then, I had only read about this in books and watched it in translated Christmas specials on television.

"Look, I'm smoking!" I giggled at my little sister, who also laughed and pretended to hold a cigarette.

With a glance that was worth a thousand words, Mami signaled for us to keep quiet. I had forgotten her instructions to us not to speak unless in private or when absolutely necessary. We had to avoid singling ourselves out. My smiling face was instantly transformed into a tight-lipped mask, silent and annoyed. But Mami was right. Although we had not left Mexico City, and our tourist visas were perfectly valid there, she would take no chances in drawing attention to ourselves. Our birthplace would have been obvious if our distinct Salvadoran accents escaped our mouths.

We continued to walk silently toward the Basilica. I was freezing. I had my arms crossed in my red satin jacket. I had even stretched the striped elastic cuffs over my clenched fists. I had picked this jacket out from one of the boxes Mami brought to El Salvador only a few weeks earlier. She had brought mostly clothing this last time, concerned that we should have enough U.S.-made clothes to bring on the trip. I had not chosen the jacket for its functionality, it had soft, flowing sleeves that danced with the slightest breeze, but it did nothing to keep me warm.

My feet began to grow cold in my new *Bracos*. I bent down my face to look at the yellow trim on my bright blue sneakers, with the sides unattractively burnt. I was trying to figure out where the cold breeze was entering my shoes to freeze my toes so. Although walking kept us a little warm, I still felt cold, wishing to get there already, wherever we were going. Suddenly, we hit a wall of people...men, women, and children, talking, laughing and eating all around.

Mariachi bands played at every corner, singing tunes to the beloved *Virgen Morena*, the dark virgin. With hardly enough breathing room amidst the crowd, we walked holding each other's hands to try to stay together. We climbed up a long stairway through the tall, iron gates of the historic church. Unable to reach its open doors, we caught only a glimpse of the Virgin's magnificent image over the sea of people congregated inside. I searched in the crowd for anyone dressed in traditional indigenous outfits, like the ones we had worn so many years in El Salvador to celebrate this holiday. Back home, we had worn colorful dresses with ribbons braided into our hair while the boys wore white cotton shirts and pants, leather sandals, and red handkerchiefs around their necks. On this occasion so many miles from home, only ordinary people in everyday clothes attended the midnight mass.

The air was thick with the spirit of the people. The glow of the countless candles flickered on the arched walls inside. The humming of the prayers streamed out in waves to the less fortunate ones, who were crammed outside the doors, like us. We held hands and poured all our faith into a single prayer, whispered on the very spot where the Aztec man Juan Diego stood, centuries before, witnessing the image of the Virgin Mary. We reluctantly headed back down the crowded steps to the square below.

We continued to roam the plaza, breathing in the cold air and walking into one blunt culture shock after another. It was hard to hear Mami's voice over the music and the chatter. The heavy *Distrito Federal* accents of the crowds around us, the accents that I had only heard in Mexican movies, echoed in my half-frozen ears. Food carts lined the streets, serving tacos and tortas with more varieties of hot sauces and jalapeños than I ever imagined possible. The air was thick with the aroma of roasted chili peppers. Even toddlers had their food smothered with the glowing red and green sauces. Although my family always had an affinity to hot and spicy food, it was never anything like this. The music, food, and celebration was supposed to last throughout the next two days but we could not stay. We walked around some more before returning to the bus station where we would leave for *Guadalajara* first thing in the morning. We spent the next few hours dozing off safely on benches inside the station, camouflaged among the hundreds of travelers, worshippers, visitors, and merchants in town for the holiday. Mami kept watch over us as we slept, figuring she might get some sleep on the bus the next morning, but I doubt she did.

The next morning we boarded our next bus for the ride to Guadalajara. As Mami found out, the three young men who accompanied us to the cathedral the night before were also on their way to the U.S. They had plans to travel by sea from Veracruz to Florida. They tried to convince her to go along, realizing that her knowledge and experience would be helpful to them. But our trip had been carefully planned long before, and our destination could not be changed. We never found out if the young men made it over. We only knew that they left Mexico City that morning on a Veracruz-bound train, without us.

NIGHTFALL

I opened my eyes and, for a moment, I had no idea where I was. The motel bed was crowded — my three sisters and I were sprawled out every which way. Mami was sitting on the same spot at edge of the bed where she was when I fell asleep the night before. Her blinkless stare was wrought with fatigue and worry. She was holding the old leather-bound bible my grandmother gave her so many years before. She turned toward me and embraced me with her smile. She had not slept since we left San Salvador two days earlier but always managed to find a smile to comfort us.

We had arrived in Guadalajara the previous morning. We spent most of the day trying to locate a friend of a friend, the priest of a local church who had offered his help should we need it during the trip. We found the church, but did not find him. We spent the night at a small motel in town and awoke to a fast-paced morning.

Our *Mexicali*-bound train departed from the Guadalajara station at noon of Day Four. I would have been a bit more excited had I known that Mexicali is at the Mexican border with California. North, South, East, West, it all feels the same after a few hours with a vinyl bus seat attached to your behind. The conductor showed us to our two cabins on a long train hall lined with plush red carpet... My mother shared very few details about the trip with us, so the first-class train tickets were a pleasant surprise. We split into two cabins across from each other. Mom took Milady and Sonia, who at eighteen was old enough to watch over us, took Daysi and me. I felt excited to have our own private space.

We put our bags in the corner and sat in the booth by the window. The small pull-down mattresses were concealed in the polished wooden walls, just as the toilet was concealed inside an inconspicuous chair. The repetitive clicking of the train over its rails filled the silence and kept us company. I wondered when I would see my grandparents in Santa Maria again.

Growing up back home, my sisters and I anxiously awaited our annual Easter visits at Mama Lidia and Papa Chepe's home, in tranquil Santa Maria. A dozen of my cousins were there one night with my sisters and me, gathered around the gigantic hammock on the porch. We talked and shared fantastic folk tales about the monstrous *Ciguanaba* and her wild escapades turning men crazy.

Papa Chepe had built that old brick house years before, equipped with electricity, unlike many of their neighbors. We could not see the emergency water well behind the house from our chosen spot at the front porch. The well is where the coconut trees end and Papa Chepe's orange grove begins. Nor could we see the stunning greenery of the surrounding volcanoes as they mixed into the horizon with the trees and the clouds above. The dirt path running from the porch to the road into town slowly blended into the grassy yard as the last traces of the afternoon sun disappeared. We were just far enough from the adobe kitchen not to detect the scent of Mama Lidia's clay water pots. We could hardly even see the outhouse just a few steps away. Within a few minutes, a blanket of silver moonlight wrapped the entire house, revealing my cousins' bright eyes. Our shadows were sharply defined on the blue walls of the porch. One by one, we filled the hammock from the center out, squeezing into the edges. We all wanted to rest our exhausted feet from the full day of running and playing and swimming in the nearby stream. The bottom of the hammock sagged so low that our behinds grazed the floor when we gently swung back and forth. I smiled to myself as I remembered this. The rocking of the train car finally made me doze off for a while.

I walked into Mami and Milady's cabin across the hall just before nightfall. A gorgeous sunset with shades of pink, orange, and red shone through their window. I asked when we would arrive in Mexicali. Mom replied that we would get there at midnight the next day. Another late night was forthcoming. Mami instructed us not to set foot out of our cabins without her. So we sat in our cabin the rest of the night no longer enjoying a bright landscape, but a pitch-black desert night through our window. We pulled the mattresses down from the wall, one for Sonia and the other for Daysi and me. We put out the light and tossed and turned in the tiny beds until we fell asleep.

"Ding! Ding! Ding!"

The soft bell that rang outside our door quickly faded but managed to snatch me from a dream I can't recall. It was just after eight a.m. Mami soon stepped in our cabin with Milady. "Come on, wash up, that's our breakfast call," she said. I did not pay attention to her eyes but I was sure that she did not sleep that night either. We got ready and walked down the carpeted hall of our train car to the dining room car. Mami ordered our mid-morning meal and softly, told us to eat enough to hold us until dinner. When we returned to our cabins with stuffed stomachs, Sonia, Daysi, and I found ourselves bored out of our minds in our tiny room. We eventually took a nap, assuming Mami and Milady would do the same.

As we slept, two immigration officers knocked on Mom's cabin door across the hall. After seeing our null tourist visas for Mexico City, they demanded money. The standard "price" for a *mordida,* or bribe, was about one hundred dollars a head, but Mami did not have nearly that much. She offered them some of her jewelry and most of the little cash she had left. They accepted the bribe and left. She came into our cabin later and told us very matter-of-factly what happened. We did not step out of our cabins again. She told us that we should be prepared for problems like this and to expect them again before our trip was over.

Mami reminded us about her coaching before leaving El Salvador, about the corrupt immigration officers. She repeated that no dream, no destination, no goal was worth risking our self-respect. Being a woman, she knew all too well, and had taught us, that these men are not always interested in money, but may demand sexual favors instead. This was one of the rare situations in which Mami allowed herself to discuss anything remotely related with sex, without feeling like she was condoning it. She did not sugarcoat this potential for violence, for rape. Only our lives were more precious than our virginity. The culprits never cared how old or how young their targets might be. She knew we might become separated anywhere along the trip.

"Run, if you can" she said, "run as fast as you can and scream as loud as you can. Find a church or the police to help you." The police might be the ones from whom we must run.

We only stepped out of our train cabin once more for an early dinner that evening and retreated once again. The next day came and went. Mami left us only minutes at a time to retrieve food from the dining car for us to eat in privacy. During her short trips to the dining car, she befriended an older Mexican couple, a husband and wife traveling with their two young boys. They had agreed to help us get a hotel room in town before they continued their own trip. Mami hoped to hide us from the hotel staff to avoid calling attention to our large group. As soon as night fell again, I knew we were close to Mexicali.

It was close to midnight again and the train screeched to a stop. My sisters and I still did not know where we were headed, but Mom seemed to be totally in control. The family Mami befriended walked with us for a couple of blocks. It was even colder than our night at the cathedral in Mexico City. We found a two-story hotel with a blue neon sign perched vertically along its side. The hotel office faced the small corner parking lot, where a single car sat beneath the streetlight. My three sisters and I waited across the street with Mom's lady friend. Mami walked up to the office window with the gentleman to check out a room for two. Once they returned with a room key, she thanked the couple profusely and they left.

We snuck into the room by taking the stairwell furthest from the office. Even in the darkness, we could see the aged stains on the concrete steps and the chipping paint on the metal rails. The thick floral drapes of our room were drawn and would stay that way throughout our stay. We kept all the lights off except for the old lamp hanging over the table by the window, and secured our door with chain and lock. Mom sat at the small table, bathed in dim yellow light, thinking, worrying. We would wait here until morning, when our coyota would escort us to Tijuana. My uncles and aunts in Los Angeles had arranged it. My sisters and I lay there awake on the crowded mattress, pretending to sleep, too scared to say a word.

First thing in the morning of Day Six, Mami rushed down to the pay phone in the hotel lobby to call her brother in L.A. She went down the front stairwell leading directly to the hotel office. The office door was propped open even at this early hour. The tiny lobby had no windows or pictures on the walls. The old payphone was so close to the counter that it was impossible to keep the clerk from eavesdropping. Mom tried to focus on a rip on the worn brown carpet to avoid eye contact with the man behind the counter. She dialed the operator to connect her with Los

Angeles. She told our relatives the name of the hotel where we were staying and casually asked about the coyota's arrival, speaking "in code," of course. Payment was a big concern. Mami was careful not to discuss money too directly. The coyota, a Tijuana woman named Amparo, was supposed to come that morning, but she did not.

During her second phone conversation with L.A. that afternoon, Mami found out that our lady guide could not come until the evening of the next day. This was a day and a half of hiding that she had not anticipated. She was high in stress and low in cash. She tried desperately to conceal our presence by never letting us leave the room, but it was impossible to hide ourselves all that well. We stayed put in our room, pacing all day, nervous, tired, and hungry. We peered out of the corner of the shut drapes, watching Mami make lightning trips to the food cart across the street, to buy a few tacos for us to eat. She came back with a dozen tiny carne asada tacos, only enough to hold us over. I barely removed the wax paper wrappings and swallowed my share of them whole, along with their abundant, cilantro-covered onions. I hated onions, but they tasted delicious that afternoon. But despite Mami's precautions, the hotel manager somehow knew that my sisters and I were hiding there. Maybe the oil-stained brown paper bags she carried, holding our precious tacos, confirmed his suspicions that she was not alone. Maybe it was her overheard long-distance calls from the lobby phone. Regardless of how he found out, he did not hesitate to act on his hunch.

Mami was an attractive thirty-five-year-old. He waited
patiently until the next morning to attack.

"How about breakfast?" he blurted at her with an
insinuating grin.   She was attempting to dial Los
Angeles for a third time. He began circling her with
his hands in his pockets, checking her out from head
to toe. Mami seriously but politely refused. She told
him she was a married woman and her husband was
upstairs waiting for her. She hung up the receiver and
left as soon as she could, avoiding any further
conversation with him. Furious, the man reached for
the phone behind the counter. Later that day, just
hours before our coyota's arrival, two Mexican
Immigration Officers came knocking.

Mami told us to make the bed while she searched
through her bags and secret pockets for all her hidden
cash.   She even took the money from the shoulder
pads of her turquoise blazer. They pounded on the
door a second time. She put the cash and a small
pouch with jewelry in her pocket, straightened her
sweater, told us to sit on the bed and headed for the
door. She quickly straightened her hair back and took
a deep breath before answering. The men stood at the
open door and demanded to see our papers.   The
officer on the right browsed through our passports and
Visas quickly and passed them on to the second
officer.   The door was still open and I could not make
out their faces against the mid-morning glare outside.
I could hardly hear what they were saying over my
pounding heart. My sisters and I sat at the edge of the
hastily made bed, immobile. I grabbed Mami's bible

from the night stand and squeezed it until I could feel the cracks in the leather cover slicing through the palm of my hand.

"These are no good," said the first man.

"Get your things and come with us," said the other forcefully.

That is when I noticed my sisters' faces, drenched with tears, like mine. Mami begged them to take the last of our money instead, but they refused, and again told us to pack and get out. I pressed my fingertip along the rusty zipper of the bible, and held on to Sonia's arm, and she held Daysi's and Daysi held Milady's. We sat there, sobbing out loud. We could not move.

The men stepped in at Mami's request, closing the door behind them. The room was all dark except for the bathroom light. Mami reached into her pocket and again offered them all of our money and every piece of gold and silver jewelry she had in the pouch. She quickly removed all her rings and necklaces and placed them in her left hand, while she held her stack of small bills wrapped with two fifties. This was hardly enough to cover a mordida for one of us, certainly not enough for five. They stood their ground despite our dramatic pleas. Mami finally told us in a stern voice, to get up. There were no sounds after that, just my pounding heart. There were no voices. I got up slowly to grab my small bag from the bathroom counter, placed the bible inside it along with all my hopes, and reluctantly zipped the bag closed. I don't know how long I stood there. The hair stuck to my cheeks did not bother me. I had to remind myself to breathe. Everything hurt.

I thought of our house, our street, our neighbors, our school, and our life in El Salvador so many miles away. I pictured the sunrise over the Duralita rooftops that I witnessed just six days before. I pictured my aunts and uncles gathered about a crowded living room kneeling in prayer for our safe arrival. And I saw my father. I pictured us returning to him, helpless, shattered. My swollen eyes finally opened at the sound of my sister's muffled cry in the darkened room.

"Give me the hundred," I heard the first officer say. She immediately rushed to the door and handed him the money. He told her to get out before others came. Then he opened the door. Daylight streamed in, blinding us all. He stood there waiting for his partner. We gasped waiting for his response. He frowned in disapproval, and hesitated, but he just glared at us and stepped outside. The first man gave us something resembling a smile and closed the door behind him. My sisters and I huddled on the bed, with our arms over each other's shoulders, the four of us trembling. Mami walked over to us and embraced us tightly with her comforting arms.

Mom rushed outside to the phone booth down the block, to call Los Angeles again. They told her to sit tight and that our coyota would be there in the afternoon. She came back to our room, tacos in hand, told us to pack and be ready to go any minute. She hung the "Do Not Disturb" sign on our doorknob and bolted the room shut. We inhaled our snack-size meal and sat on the bed to wait.

It was nearly six o'clock on the evening of Day Seven when the coyota finally arrived. Amparo was in her mid-forties, sloppily dressed. Her badly colored hair was barely brushed and was held down with gaudy barrettes. She carried an orange tote bag made of plastic mesh. She brought her eight-year-old son with her. She gave us instructions for the three-hour bus ride to her house. It was as though she and the boy had done this a million times.

"You will walk with my son" she said, pointing at Sonia and Milady. "You," pointing at Daysi and me "are with me". Mami would walk on her own. We were not to interact with anyone outside our "group" until we reached her house in Tijuana. Every "group" the advantage of a Mexican accent: Amparo's and her son's which were native, and Mami's which had been learned during her years in Los Angeles.

We left the hotel just after sunset, and not a moment too soon. It was still early but the evening was already darker than midnight. We walked in our groups along several boulevards. Most had at least four lanes each way. The road I remember most clearly had fences on either side. They were lined with political posters for the upcoming presidential election. The signs were identical and went on for miles.

"Miguel De La Madri-i-i-i-id .... Hurta-a-a-a-a-d-o-o-o-o-o!," the boy chanted at the top of his lungs.

He was walking with Milady and Sonia just behind us, engraving the name of the soon-to-be Mexican president in my memory forever. He tapped on the endless paper signs and ran his hand against the exposed chain link fence between them. His loudness made me nervous, but the streets were fairly empty. I had to fight the urge to turn around to look at the boy. It was as though he was chanting exclusively to annoy me. I don't remember how far we walked. It took us an hour to reach the bus station, where, by the grace of God, the boy finally shut up.

The coyota, her son, and Mami purchased our tickets at the booth and we boarded the ten o'clock bus to Tijuana, each "group" separated by a few strangers. We sat on different rows within sight of each other. The seats were covered with faded brown leather-like plastic, cracked around the corners. The coyota sat along the aisle with Daysi and me. Sonia and Milady sat with the boy just two rows ahead, and Mami just one row behind all of us on the left side of the bus. I tried not to be too obvious as I stared at my sisters. I squeezed Daysi's hand to keep myself from looking back at my mother. Daysi shook her hand loose after a few minutes. I had cut off her circulation. About ten minutes later, the bus was full and we began our ride to Tijuana.

After about half an hour, the bus was stopped by Police officers on a routine check. Immigration or not, uniforms posed a danger to us. The passengers instantly stopped their chattering. The only sound remaining was the thump of their boots on the floor of the bus. Three officers walked along the aisle, shining their flashlights past every face. I stared directly ahead. I tried to concentrate on the grooves of the fake leather seat in front of us. My eyes were half closed, feigning sleepiness. I thought my heart would jump straight out of my throat and land at their feet as they passed. They got off the bus, signaling to the driver to continue on his way.

We arrived in Tijuana in the early hours of Day Eight. We caught a taxicab from the bus station to Amparo's modest house. We noticed a stack of pillows and sheets on the couch, our cue that we would camp on the living room floor. The yellow carpet was old and worn in several places, but I was impressed by the fact that it was there at all. Back home, carpet was expensive and virtually unheard of, affordable only to a few of our wealthier neighbors. Cool floor tiles were a welcome comfort in a typical home.

We crashed on the living room floor for a few seconds. I could have slept for a month. I was startled awake by the racket of Amparo's children stampeding past our living room camp to the kitchen. I frowned at their lack of consideration — running around in the middle of the night. I peeked out from under my thin sheet. I spotted our disheveled escort and her jumpy family, including the chanting eight-year-old, sitting in the kitchen, awaiting breakfast. Mami and my sisters were sitting on the sofa across from me. I was the last one to get up.

"Good morning! You all up now? You want some breakfast?" the lady asked from the kitchen table.

I got up, folded my sheet, and placed it on the top of the neat stack my sisters made with theirs on the couch. We made our way to the kitchen as Mami helped to gather plates and serve food. We were famished. After Mami asked if there was any pancake mix, Amparo's kids wailed with excitement as though she meant to cook for them. Too kindhearted to say no, Mami saw herself preparing stack after stack without so much as a bit of hope to prepare some for her own daughters. Our shriveled stomachs had resigned themselves to growl hopelessly at each other in a loud and pathetic dialogue.

Mami was livid.

She finally made us sit at the table and began serving us directly from the skillet, not giving the others a chance to snatch them from the large plate in the middle of the table. As we waited to eat, I noticed the box of "Lucky Charms" cereal above the refrigerator and I smiled. The cereal box was printed in English. Amparo apologized to us for arriving late at the hotel the day before. She was obviously trying to appease Mami so that she could finish the "job" by bringing us across. The woman did not realize how much she and her children had upset Mom by treating her like a servant in the kitchen.

"This money," Amparo added, "it's for my water heater, we don't have one, you know..."

At first I hadn't the slightest clue why a water heater would be so important, but then I remembered our breath-freezing experience in Mexico City. Being that much farther north, I realized Tijuana must get much colder. The coyota pulled a plastic milk jug from the refrigerator. It was quite different from the milk we were used to in El Salvador, made from canned milk powder. We always drank milk hot. It was always sweetened when prepared, even when we poured it onto Frosted Flakes. Although ready-to-use Foremost brand milk was sold in every shop around the neighborhood, in handy little quart-size bags, it was expensive enough to be outside our budget. Amparo placed the milk jug on the table and retired to her room. She emerged an hour later and began to explain to us how we would cross the border later that day.

The coyota showed us the picture IDs we would use to cross. The lady pictured on Mami's card had long, beautiful hair and features so perfectly similar, it was uncanny. I took a look at the little girl on the second card. The little girl was huddled next to her mother in the black-and-white photograph with a tiny trace of a smile. Milady, Daysi, and I would take turns pretending to be her to cross with her mother, a local from Tijuana who obviously did this often. The girl was about my age but looked nothing like any of us aside from her dark hair. Noticing my disbelief, the coyota reassured us that it would work. Her nodding head was not reassuring in the least. No ID was found resembling Sonia. She would have to cross on foot, guided by a coyote, walking through the mountains and fields across the borderline.

Amparo brought our fake mother over to teach us details about her child: the little girl's name, her birthday, her address, the names of her brothers and sisters, her school, and her teachers, and a few other things. Mom learned similar things about her ID. The same woman would cross with Milady at the Tijuana border gate, with Daysi at Tecate border that evening, and with me back in Tijuana the next day. Mami would cross at Tecate on the same night as Daysi. We would be reunited with each other in a house in San Ysidro the next morning and with Sonia the next afternoon. Milady, Daysi and I quizzed each other. Sonia prepared herself mentally for the walk across. It all made sense and we were ready.

Mami reminded my thirteen-year-old sister that if she felt she was in any danger, she should run and scream and find help wherever she could. In a few minutes we would be separated until all of us made it across the border. Daysi verbalized everything that I knew I shouldn't ask – she did not understand why we had to split up. Mami explained that Milady would not be alone for long. We all hugged at once and Mom touched her forehead to Milady's to pray. By noon, Milady, her temporary mother, and the coyota were gone.

We waited the entire day locked up in that house. Mami paced in the living room, her brow heavy with worry. The coyote called from San Ysidro with the news that Milady crossed safely. Mami spoke to her in a reassuring voice; it was clear from our side of the conversation that Milady was nervous and scared. We waited patiently until sundown for Daysi and Mami's turn to cross at the Tecate border gates, east of Tijuana. Amparo talked Mami and Daysi through the details of their crossing again. They left by six o'clock, leaving Sonia and me in the Tijuana house with

Amparo's noisy children to wait our turn the next day. I went to sleep around nine that night, again finding my spot on the carpeted living room floor, next to my big sister. Mami startled me awake when she tried to squeeze her way into our blankets without disturbing us, several hours later. Before we could ask, Mami began to explain.

They got to the Tecate border around seven p.m. Daysi and her "mother" crossed with no questions asked, a few people ahead of Mom in line. Daysi looked back when they walked beyond the gate. She saw when the officers took my mother's ID and moved her to a different room for questioning. Nobody knew what Daysi would to do, if she would scream out or something. The coyote just pulled her away.

"My poor *pegoste*," thought my Mom.

Mami was questioned for a couple of hours. Her ID card said she lived in Tijuana but the officers did not buy her unconvincing border accent. They were, however, fooled by it enough to believe Mami was from Central Mexico. After confiscating her ID, they turned her back into the Tecate border town. It was nearly ten o'clock at night. She had no transportation and was sixty miles away from Sonia and me. She was unsure of the fate of her two daughters who had crossed the border. She had only a few Mexican pesos, the memorized address of the coyota's house, and raw determination. She approached a bus station and asking directions wherever she could, and somehow, some way, found her way back to the house. It was many hours later. She was exhausted, disappointed, and sick with worry.

The following morning marked our ninth day on the road. Daysi's temporary "Mom" backed out of the deal after Mami was caught. Unmoved by my mother's ordeal, Amparo yelled at Mami for losing her ID card. Mami, Sonia and I were officially "paper-less." A few minutes and a few frantic phone calls later, Amparo located another Tijuana woman willing to cross with me. I had to quickly relearn my "identity". The new lady came over right away to cover the details. She was a large woman, tall and heavy. I got the impression that her hugs might be capable of smothering young children. She wore a flower-printed dress and her short dark hair curled around her face. She said little, letting Amparo do most of the talking. I left the coyota's house after saying good-bye to Mami and my oldest sister.

Amparo could not find ID cards that resembled Mami and Sonia. They would be forced to walk through the border's fields and mountains together. This was actually a blessing in disguise since Sonia was only a teenager herself, and might have struggled on her own. They would start their own journey across a few minutes later.

My new "mom" and I left Amparo's house and were dropped off half a block from the Border gates. We walked up and stood in line outside the border station for a few minutes. The blaring conversations and crying babies and honking cars blended together into an annoying ringing in my ears. There were lots of women holding shopping bags like the one my "Mom" carried. Shoppers' faces blend right into the Border officers' daily routine. Terrified of forgetting any vital information, I repeated it all in my mind, pressing my lips together to keep them from moving as I practiced: who I was, where I lived, the whole thing.

We crossed by eleven a.m. Nothing was asked of me but my name. I might have sighed with relief once setting foot on the other side, but my family had never been this split apart. The lady and I walked to a second car just another half a block up. I don't even remember if it was the same car that took us there. The streets flashed uneventfully at the corners of my eyes. A single nagging thought fluttered around in my head. Mami and Sonia had begun their trek by now.

I was reunited with Milady and Daysi in San Ysidro, where we waited until late afternoon. The house was full with light and silence. We waited, sitting on a small sofa facing away from the window, drapes drawn. My sisters had spent their restless night in the same spot. It was bright outside, I think. A strange man strolled into the house – the same person who brought Milady there the day before. The three of us piled into the back seat of his car and he drove us to the parking lot of a nearby Kmart store. It was after five, so the winter sun had almost completely set. I spotted some silhouettes outlined against the stained, pink sky. Sonia and Mami appeared walking toward us. We wanted to run to greet them, but we just watched them impatiently. Their shoes were muddy, their clothes dusty, their hair disheveled, and their bodies exhausted. Sonia tried to rush to the car, but Mami held her by the arm until they reached us. I exhaled. We were together, on the other side. But we still had a long way to go.

We arrived at an apartment house in Chula Vista at six o'clock. The Tudor building was three stories high and had dark oak walls. We climbed up a winding stairwell to a unit on the top floor to prepare for our arrival in Los Angeles. We had absolutely nothing but the clothes on our backs. All our belongings remained behind, passports and all. The coyote would bring our things to my relatives' apartment in Los Angeles later on. While in Chula Vista, Mami told us about her crossing in the mountains with Sonia earlier that day.

They were dropped off with a guide off the side of a road outside Tijuana. They followed their guide onto a nearby trail. They hiked for miles using the desert brush as cover, squinting through the morning glare. They climbed up hills on overgrown trails teeming with mud and rocks. Other clusters of people walked and ran alongside them for a portion of their trek, following the same route. A woman in one of the groups held an infant in her arms and struggled to keep up. When directed by their guide, Mami and my sister ran full speed for about half an hour that lasted an eternity. Sonia was close to fainting. They had walked for nearly four hours with no water to drink or a moment's rest. Mami put her arm around Sonia's waist to propel her forward. They eventually arrived at a desolate road, God knows where. An old beat up car was waiting for them to drive them to our busy meeting spot, half an hour away. We knew there was much more to it, perhaps things that were too hard for them to relive and for us to witness, so they did not share more. I did not dare ask if they had been left alone, if they had been lost, or what else they may have seen. I could not bear to know.

Our group was too large to be driven together to Los Angeles together. Mami decided to go first with Daysi and myself, leaving Sonia and Milady in the Chula Vista apartment house overnight. The coyote would drive them first thing in the morning. Mami prepared to leave with Daysi and myself. She carefully washed her face, cleaned up her shoes, straightened up our hair, and shook out the dirt from our clothes. We would be riding in a car to L.A. with the man who drove us to Kmart. We could not afford to attract any undue attention. She prepped Sonia and Milady again, heeding the same warnings about their safety and their priorities. Mami, Daysi, and I reluctantly departed around six thirty, leaving my two sisters behind. I looked intently at my sisters' faces precisely as we left, struggling to engrave them into my head, but my heart refused to record such a painful parting.

All I can recall about that moment are the dark wooden walls of the strange apartment house.

LIGHTS

At dusk, six days before Christmas, we had to ride unnoticed through the border checkpoint in San Onofre. We drove on the northbound interstate, leaving Chula Vista and my two older sisters behind. The coyote was trained to make the white sedan blend in with traffic — the car had current California plates, it was not too dirty and not too clean. He even had a way to make us disappear from view. We slowed down and pulled off the freeway north of San Diego. He drove into a quiet Oceanside neighborhood, and explained that we would be traveling inside the trunk of the car.

My parents had tried to prepare us for something like this. Two weeks before our trip, they took us to see a film about a twelve-year-old boy attempting to cross the border to meet his mother, who worked as a housekeeper in California. The boy rode with a coyote in the cabin of the truck that was carrying a dozen others in the back. They were pulled over by a patrol car on a desolate road in the middle of the night. The officer asked the driver and the boy to step out and open the back. When the driver opened the back door, another coyote fired a shotgun, killing the officer and accidentally shooting the boy on the arm. The boy's injury wasn't fatal but the coyote wouldn't carry a wounded person. The coyote stood over the boy, mouthed the words "I'm sorry," as he shot him in the chest. The boy was dead. When we got home, my parents explained that we would run this risk too.

The coyote pulled into a dimly lit alley and into the carport of an apartment building, hidden from view. He parked and stepped out to the back of the car. Mom looked over her shoulder from the passenger seat and nodded at my little sister and me. It was time to go. As we stepped out, my stomach fluttered with nerves. I squeezed my mother's arm and started to feel better. A gust of wind blew hair into my eyes. That is when I realized that my hands were fused onto my mother's. I looked over at my sister Daysi, clinging to Mom's other arm, her bright brown eyes wide open and her hair a bit disheveled by the chilly breeze. It was like looking in the mirror. He opened the trunk. It was spacious and empty, lined with navy carpet. His instructions were brief.

"You can talk if you wish, and even move around if you need to, as long as you can hear the radio playing," he said.

When we reached the freeway checkpoint, fourteen miles north, he would turn off the radio. That would be our signal to keep absolutely quiet and still, especially when we slowed down to a stop. At that time, border patrol officers would be standing inches from us. The slightest move could expose us. He even suggested breathing slowly. Mami stepped in first and positioned herself between us so she could hold on to us both.

"It will be okay," he reassured us as he closed the door and wrapped us in darkness.

Daysi and I remained perfectly still, holding on to our mother as if we would need less air that way. He turned the radio on, started the car, and we were off.

Threads of light from the street lamps flickered through the crevices around the trunk door and lit up the tiny keyhole. It was dark in there. We were free to talk as long as the radio played, but we did not utter a word to each other. I strained to pull my thoughts away from terrible images of people who died all the time trying to make their way to the United States. Instead, I tried to make sense of the commercial jingles and holiday songs still playing on the radio. The car accelerated and decelerated and turned several times. We rolled around a bit. Sacrifices and priorities, I could hear Mami think. Sacrifices and priorities.

After twenty minutes that took an eternity, the car began to slow down. Then the music was gone. I turned my head and buried it under Mami's arm, shut my eyes and held my breath, as Daysi did. The silence was infinite. The car rolled to a stop. The tiny points of light shining into our hiding place threatened to give us away.

A strange man's voice.

The man asked a question in English. The coyote responded briefly with words I could not understand. Oh, God, I have to sneeze. My eyes were still shut and my lungs struggled for air, as I held my breath. The car began to move. Will the officer call him back? Will they ask him to open the trunk? Instead, the car slowly rolled away. The coyote turned on the radio, our signal that it was all okay. But I had forgotten how to move. Mami shook my arm to let me know I could open my eyes. The lights flickering through the cracks around the trunk door were comforting. "The faster they flicker," I thought, "the faster we will get to

Los Angeles." The car began to slow down again, but the music was still playing on the radio.

We stopped abruptly and we heard a car door open and slam shut. The man opened the door and light poured from the street lamp above into every corner of our hiding spot. It was about eight o'clock and already very dark out in San Clemente. I stepped out and stood with my arms interlocked together, squinting at Mami and Daysi as they got out. I smiled at them. Daysi smiled back but there was no smile on Mami's face. Her other two daughters were still alone in a strange house, miles away. She shuffled Daysi and me into the back seat and sat up front without a word.

The next two and a half hours flew right past me. I noticed the green freeway signs from my seat behind the driver. I made it a game to see how many I could pronounce. San Juan Capistrano. Oso. La Paz. Alicia. Laguna. El Toro. Costa Mesa. Santa Ana. Cerritos. The urban cityscape grew before my eyes until billboards and overpasses and railroad tracks surrounded us. Many signs around us bore unpronounceable English text. Then, eventually, we saw it emerge.

"That is Downtown Los Angeles", Mami said with a brush of excitement.

The lit buildings soared up to the heavens. I stretched my neck as far as I could to peek through the windshield from the backseat. My stubborn heart had once again found its way to my throat and my stomach quivered with a vengeance. We drove past the downtown skyline, pulled off the freeway, and turned left at Union Avenue — the street on my uncles' address!

We turned into a parking lot. The English sign on the shop next door had several words, but the unmistakable word "LIQUOR" was lit up the brightest. My sister and I clutched each other's hands, frozen with excitement. Mami melted us apart with the warmest smile she had worn since we left El Salvador. She took us by the hand and we walked up to my uncles' place. The night was crisp but our hearts were warm with anticipation. The hilly avenue was packed densely with the brick façades and fire escapes of old apartment houses. A narrow strip of cloudy December sky peeked through the top of the buildings and the rows of barren trees. Mami rushed up the stairs to the second floor, with us closely behind. She knocked on the door. The loud talking inside stopped instantly and the door swung open. In an instant we were swept inside with embraces and kisses and Alleluias. Happy faces flashed past me that I would recognize anywhere. Tía Melba. Tío Jose. Tío Salomon. Tío Hildo. Tía Betty. Tío German. Tía Tita. More than twenty people packed the tiny apartment. Several people were still kneeling in prayer. We were there and we were safe but not all quite home.

Daysi and I collapsed on the bed a few minutes later despite the loud chatter in the room. When I woke up a few hours later, Mami and my uncles and aunts were still talking. Morning poured in through the single window facing east, but it did not seem to be blinding anyone but me. My two older sisters were due in any second. The minutes dragged on for years.

My mind started wandering into visions of my sisters in that strange house in Chula Vista, of them huddled in the dark trunk of a car, of corrupt officers, of cruel coyotes, of border patrol helicopters, search lights, sirens...

Knock, knock, knock.

I wanted to swing the door open myself this time, but someone beat me to it. We made it. Tears were as abundant as smiles. As soon as the five of us were together, Mami gave us the good news: My father had begun his own trip and was due in L.A. in a couple of days. We drove to our apartment in the San Fernando Valley and began the countdown to his arrival.

.   .   .

A few short days after we kissed him good-bye at the bus station in San Salvador, my father started his own journey to California. His retirement pension had been processed unexpectedly fast. Unbeknownst to us, he had the money to travel and left El Salvador we had made it to the other side.

Papi left El Salvador with a group of six others and a coyote. The coyote was a Salvadoran man in his early twenties, named Evelio. He charged them $1200 each to guide them from San Salvador to Ciudad Juarez and across the border to El Paso, Texas. He ran a few trips like this each year. Evelio bought them bus tickets to Guatemala and then to Mexico City warning them never stand together but to always stay within sight of each other. Dad was the oldest in the group at thirty-eight, the one woman and five other men were all in their mid to late twenties. After arriving in Mexico City, he took the group to a hotel where he left them for hours, with no food or money, while he drank himself into a stupor. Papi snuck down to the lobby to phone our relatives in L.A., clearing his throat to disguise the occasional grumble of his stomach. Evelio stumbled into the hotel room much later and passed out on the floor, where he greeted morning with the hangover of the century.

The group headed for the bus station to board a Chihuahua-bound bus. Dad's group dispersed strategically across the floor as their drowsy coyote lined up at the ticket booth. He did not notice the out-of-uniform officers eyeing the group. Only thirty minutes before the train's scheduled arrival, my dad watched in dismay as his travel companions were pulled aside one by one by the officers. One of the men in the group, pretending to read a newspaper, slowly slipped off while the arrests continued. Papi was eventually caught himself. The group was gathered and, together with the officers, they watched an ill Evelio come out of the bathroom holding his head. The guards expected that he was just another member of the group, certainly not the leader. When he finally appeared, Evelio produced the mordida that the officers demanded, just about five minutes before their bus departed. After hasty instructions on where to go at the end of the ride, they rushed in. Their brief stay in Mexico City had come to an end.

Their bus arrived in Chihuahua after a long journey. Without so much as a night's rest, they boarded a packed mid-morning train to the border town of Ciudad Juarez. Their train to Juarez was full. The group disappeared into the crowd like old pros but they were still singled out at several points along the train route. However, whenever anyone approached them, Evelio stood up and gestured to the officer. After a brief exchange, the officer left the car without incident, or confrontation. Bizarre as it was, it was a well-orchestrated ballet. My father stood in the crowded coach car clutching the handle overhead for the four-hour ride to the border, with nothing on his mind but his daughters' faces and Evelio's earlier instructions.

"The safe house is about a mile from the station. It's gray, with a chicken-wire fence around the front. You will split into two groups of two, one on each side of the street."

"You," he pointed at Papi, "will walk on your own. And I will lead ahead with her," he said, winking at the nervous young woman.

And they were off. They walked through a "squatter" neighborhood, with unpaved roads and sparse rows of cheap-looking homes, the kind that looks old after just about a year. Papi's heart pounded faster as he spotted the safe house around a corner. That may be why, at first, he did not hear the unmarked patrol car screech to a stop behind them. There were no badges, no warrants, no government seals. Just one man, calling out to them. The man ordered the entire group into a van and took them to a parking lot a couple of miles away. He held them at gunpoint and took the last of Evelio's bribe stash. After the robber drove away, Evelio took the group into the "safe" house. The room added to the back of the house with two bare, stained mattresses on the floor would be their resting spot for the next half day. That very night, the group crossed. The few possessions they had carried since San Salvador stayed in the Juarez house as they moved on.

They left the house at ten p.m. to go into town. Evelio handed the group over to another coyote and left. His job was done. A car took them to a spot two hundred yards from the Río Grande, where they were split into two groups. The first group walked to the water's edge and swam across. My father's trio climbed on top of a large pipe across a narrow spot of the river. They held on to the ridged metal pipe with their arms around it. They crawled along the rough surface, wiping off grime, rust, and cobwebs with their clothes. They jumped over an eight-foot chain link fence to land in El Paso, Texas. They walked to a hotel they could see from the fence. Someone awaited them there, in an old green sedan for their one-hour ride to San Antonio.

They were dropped off in front of San Antonio City Hall just after midnight. Homeless people lined the sidewalk where they ended up. No one was there waiting for them. They paced trying to separate themselves from each other, trying not to stand out by standing together. A station wagon with an unfamiliar driver finally drove up with the rest of the group and hurriedly signaled them in. They rode to a nearby hotel where they would get ready for their final ride into Los Angeles at dawn.

The green sedan ahead escorted them as their van left San Antonio. This man would warn them by radio if they needed to detour ahead, to avoid officers or any other danger. They had to turn several times during their eighteen-hour ride to Southern California. My father's curly hair wore a layer of dust. But he was anxious to see his wife and four daughters. They arrived in our Valley apartment early the next morning. I awoke to his beautiful smile surrounded by days' worth of stubble. The frown he wore when I last saw him had completely disappeared. In the following moments, our small apartment gave way to an explosion of laughter, screams, and tears. Even as we squeezed into Mom's tiny apartment, overwhelmed by debt, things finally began to feel right for us.

LESSONS

"...*And now here he is...Strong enough to bend records with his bare hands, able to tell tall tales in a single breath... It's SUPER-DEES, yes, SUPER-DEES! Mild-mannered disc-jockey and morning entertainer fights a never-ending battle for truth, justice, and the pursuit of loose women...*"

Snooze. Is it morning already?

"...*That was Men At Work with 'Who Can it Be Now?' as we get close to the top of the hour on this CHILLY Tuesday morning. If you need to be there by 6 o'clock, you only have ten minutes left, but the freeways are wide open all over the Southland. Bring out the sweater today, we expect a high of 50 degrees in Downtown L.A, and ONLY 45 in the Valleys...And coming up here on KIIS-FM 102.7, we have Rod Stewart asking all you 'Young Hearts' out there, to c'mon and be free tonight...*"

Double snooze. I cherished those last ten minutes after my sisters got up for their showers and I had the queen bed all for myself. We traded this precious shift, bartered with it, longed for it. A carefully planned shower schedule allowed all nine of us to use the one bathroom every morning without traffic jams. We had tripled the population of my mother's two-bedroom apartment overnight. With so many people sharing so little space, privacy was a rare commodity.

Mami had been living in that sunny, two-story building with my uncles, Edgardo and Donel, for some time. The place was barren at first, missing even the basics we had in El Salvador. Just before going to El

Salvador to get us, Mom had replaced her old twin mattress with a queen bed for my sisters and me to share. Eventually, closets overflowed with treasures from garage sales, dime stores, and clearance racks at Zody's. We shopped at local thrift stores long before "vintage" was fashionable. Soon enough, every inch of brown shag carpet in the place was used for something. Mom assigned the kitchen cupboards to protect my uncles' food from our alarming appetites. Even the area above the yellow refrigerator was replete with boxes of cereal and canned food.

Mami immediately resumed her work routine, doubled or tripled at times, working days both at a deli and a military surplus shop. At night, she managed the Jack-In-The-Box down the street. My sisters and I walked the two blocks to the restaurant to see her during her night shift breaks if they were early enough. She fed us apple turnovers and orange juice and asked us about our day. We were normally asleep when she made it back home and she had little time to spend with us in her daily struggle to catch up, but we understood.

My father began looking for work right away, but searched for weeks without success. He spent entire days waiting at a day-laborer meeting point, just outside a lumberyard in town. They called the place *Las Piedras* because of the large jagged rocks next to the sidewalk. The men came to Las Piedras every morning hoping to find an employer for the day, no work was too rough, no day too long, no place too far, no wage too low. Their worn baseball caps did little to relieve their scalps from the heat or the cold. The men waited tirelessly, despite disgusted looks from passing cars. The men returned religiously, even if they had been conned into working for no pay, or if vindictive neighbors had triggered Immigration raids that they narrowly escaped. They often left with empty hands, with nothing but their will to return the next dawn. Papi, who seldom had luck at Las Piedras, eventually got a job at the factory where Mami used to work.

•   •   •

We visited with my aunts and uncles in L.A. every weekend at first. Tío Jose showed up early Saturday mornings to pick us up — I didn't bother hitting the snooze button on the alarm clock on those days. We quickly learned the correct coin combinations for the bus fare, even though dimes were the size of *pesetas* and quarters were the size of the nickels we knew. I memorized the multiple bus routes from our Valley apartment to the Pico Union District by heart. During the two-hour bus trek, we took in L.A. life: the crowds, the traffic, the freeway systems, 7-11 stores, automated banks, drive-through restaurants, dry cleaners, shopping centers, and rotating orange spheres at Unocal gas stations. Without a car, we could not know it was in fact a thirty-minute drive. Tío Jose, Tío Hildo, and Tío Salomon took turns making this bus expedition every few days to escort us on our daytrips, and repeated the journey to return us home, sometimes the next day.

Tía Betty took us to the massive Boys Supermarket on Vermont Avenue — my first grocery shopping experience... It was colder than the Arctic in that store. Cold milk was sold in plastic jugs and tortillas were thinner than paper. We found at least eighty-seven types of cookies and more frozen food than I could count. Tía Betty walked us past the perfect fruits and vegetables so colorful and shiny, they could have been made of wax. She pointed out the peanut butter jars and explained that it could be served on sandwiches with jelly. Disgusting. We loaded our groceries onto a round moving platform that moved toward the cashier at the touch of a button. I was mesmerized.

Tía Melba took us for a walk along Wilshire Boulevard in Beverly Hills. Every window display glittered with Christmas spirit. Every light pole was clad with elaborate silver garlands and wreaths, sparkling with silver and gold. This is what Mami had wished for us to see all those Christmases she could not share with us.

Tío Jose and Tío Hildo sat with us on the grassy hills of MacArthur Park, where we relaxed some Saturday afternoons if the wait for their building's coin-operated laundry was too long.

Even the mild Southern California winter weather shocked our systems. My first jacket was a most welcome addition to my growing wardrobe. I wore that blue hooded coat long after my arms had outgrown the sleeves. Change was all around us, but the most obvious and terrifying change was English. English, everywhere.

Our first day of school came. Mom took Milady and me to Christopher Columbus Junior High School, at the heart of suburbia, to enroll in the eighth grade.

Mr. Lehman, the Columbus English-as-a-Second-Language counselor, put Milady and me through an informal English verbal test.

"Good morning."

"Good mor-neen," we both responded.

"What is your name?"

"My name ees EH-beh-leen."

He turned to my sister.

"And what is your name?"

"My name ees Mee-LAH-dee."

We grinned at Mami, who smiled proudly.

"How old are you, Evelyn?"

Silence.

"Milady, how old are you?"

We both looked down in shame. Mami was still smiling, though, that made us feel better.

Mr. Lehman placed Milady and me into the most introductory ESL track offered at the school. He put us back into the seventh grade, although we had just completed it in El Salvador, thinking we might be better off spending the extra semester learning the language. Mr. Lehman's routine decision was one of the most crucial turning points of my life.

The first few days felt artificial, like a dream. I had no use for my voice. I was left out of entire conversations, out of entire days. I had no words for my non-Spanish speaking classmates, for my non-ESL teachers, for the clerks at the attendance office, for the cafeteria workers serving me lunch everyday. I felt distant, like these people who were there to help me could never relate to me. They probably had never drank coconut water, or eaten a real hand-made tortilla or a mango right off the tree. They probably never heard Pedro Infante sing and would not even recognize Chespirito if they were staring right into his silly, freckled superhero face. In my classrooms, even my own foreign classmates did not understand my innate urge to stand whenever a teacher entered the room, as I had done since Kindergarten, to show the respect all teachers deserve.

Our school days of morning or afternoon "shifts" in El Salvador were long gone. School days were endless. We had a long list of new school rules, swarms of students, and no school uniforms. How could we afford to wear something different every single day? This could not possibly be real life.

Eventually, I began to feel comfortable in a very small circle of friends, Spanish-speaking only, of course.

First period: Physical Education. Code for Cruel and Unusual Punishment. The changing of clothes in the locker room was only the beginning. I had never been comfortable changing in front of my own sisters, and the four of us shared a bedroom all our lives. My generic tennis shoes, second-hand corduroy pants, and glittery-decal t-shirts looked even plainer next to our classmates' Jordache jeans, designer Esprit blouses, and those trendy rubber sandals in colors to match every outfit. Their elaborate make-up and sculpted feathered hairdos made my flat hair and chocolate-flavored lip-gloss look even more juvenile.

After the torture chamber, P.E. class lined up outside. We sat on the handball courts where the teacher gave her instructions for the day. Our teacher spoke only English. Even if we had friends to translate for us, talking was forbidden. There were new instructions for every sport, new words with no extra explanations, certainly nothing in writing, and no chance to ask questions. We understood the object of some of the games: volleyball, basketball, softball... But Flag Football? Badminton? Nothing made any sense.

For many days at first, Milady sat at the back of those lines, frustrated, with her back hunched over and her long legs crossed on the cold asphalt. She sat, confused, wearing half a smirk and half a frown, feeling uncomfortable in the scratchy blue gym shorts that hovered about her waist like a static polyester bubble. She sat, pretending to understand every word the teacher said.

"Blah, blah, blah-blah-blah. All right? Blah, blah, blah."

My sister sat quietly, just a few feet from me, feeling the same distress that I did. Each word was heavier than the last, a burden on her mind, and mine. After the mumbling ended, we followed the group along and depended on others to, quite literally, point us in the right direction. We stumbled our way through most P.E. mornings for quite a while.

Time would do away with the stiffness and discomfort of those scratchy gym shorts, but this kind of transition is always a bit tougher on the fabric of the soul.

One morning, Milady and I decided that we were not quite up to joining P.E. class. We chose instead to get familiar with our campus. The grounds were much more massive than any campus we had ever attended. We were half an hour into our excursion when...

"Why are you girls not in class?" the school "Nark" shouted. Luckily he understood Spanish.

"Oh, we didn't feel like attending P.E. today. We'll show up at our next class, though. For sure."

Never did it dawn on us that attendance was not optional. In El Salvador, participating in class is a privilege, treasured by those fortunate enough to not have to work to support their families in their childhood. A student might be sent home from school over the slightest infraction: arriving late, disrespecting a teacher, not paying attention, even a wrinkled or dirty uniform, depending on the school. So there we were, confronted with our first truancy, completely unaware that we had done anything wrong. We learned our lesson quickly that day.

Second through Sixth Periods: *English-as-a Second-Language.* Code for Independent Study. The teacher assigned English workbooks with reading and writing exercises for each student to complete at their own pace. Most classmates in my ESL classroom reverted back to their native languages to chit-chat in class. Conversations in Spanish, Chinese, Farsi, Korean, Tagalog, and Vietnamese rang all around. Meanwhile, some of us completed our workbooks on our own, while the teacher read magazines at her desk. It was easy to see why many of my newfound friends had been stuck in the same level of learning for years. Even the most devoted of teachers found themselves overwhelmed and pinned to the wall, ill-equipped to overcome a single culture or language barrier much less seven or eight at once.

ESL Math was the Arithmetic Graveyard, where immigrant children's math skills were brought to die, no matter how brilliant their performance or potential. We learned to expect little from our teachers, who already seemed to expect very little from us.

Lunch Period. Code for Relief. Every day, when the lunch bell rang, we put our books away. The shedding of the books was a ritual totally new to me. My seventh grade locker was the first tiny space ever assigned specifically to me, not to be shared by anyone, not even my sisters. I was definitely swimming in uncharted waters. Once book-free, my classmates and I took our weekly meal tickets and exchanged them for pepperoni-deficient pizza, or burritos with melted cheese oozing out of the ends, or french fries and cheeseburgers that made the ketchup and mustard look especially bright.

All my Spanish-speaking classmates had blue meal tickets like mine. Most of them had but a few cents allowance each day, if at all. The tickets were a fact of life. Exchanging them for lunch was as routine as the moving in herds from class to class every fifty minutes. At first, I never wondered why many recent immigrants had the tickets too, and why some kids paid to eat the school's food, or brought their own lunches. It was a while before I understood the concept of welfare — we hardly had the right to complain. Nevertheless, we went on with our daily rite of mingling and whining and picking at the food on the plate. If we needed something to top off the meal, we recruited our more fluent classmates to venture out of our Spanish-only haven. They went up to the window and bought the Corn Nuts or the extra coffee cake to soothe our cravings. If only for a few minutes during the day, we had a way around our constant need to practice English.

That spring, my school held its annual International Evening and Talent Show, the first campus event my parents ever attended. It was a celebration of the school's cultural diversity and of the achievements in the ESL program. My fellow classmates came to the auditorium wearing faces I had never seen before. The shyest of students, the ones who barely said a word in my basic ESL class, glowed with joy and spoke uninterruptedly amidst their families in their native tongues. Many came wearing traditional dress and many honored the banquet table with their best homemade dishes. Milady and I put down the tray of *pasteles* that Mami had prepared. The potluck table was decorated with a gorgeous array of exotic cuisine. The hall was filled with the sounds of cultural poetry, music, and dance performed by my very friends: elegant Vietnamese fan dancing, cheerful Mexican Folklórico. A Korean classmate, the quietest of girls, strolled delicately to the piano, clad with a pink ruffled dress and buckled patent leather shoes. Soft pink barrettes held her hair carefully in place. She sat down, and in a swift stroke of the keys, tore into a classic Mozart piano concerto that captivated everyone within earshot.

That night I ventured outside my comfort circle, my Spanish-haven, for the first time. I began to see myself as part of a larger picture.

Back at home, I spent every free moment listening to the radio. I tape-recorded songs I liked so I could play them over and over. I lay on my stomach on the bed, with a prehistoric boom box right beside me on the comforter. I had paper and pen in hand and used my dad's huge yellow headphones, which doubled the size of my head. I played my homemade tapes line by line, playing and pausing, playing and pausing, stopping to write what I heard, until I had every word of every song jotted down and memorized. The sounds of Hall and Oates, Laura Branigan, Devo, Earth, Wind & Fire, Run DMC, and Michael Jackson, bounced off the bedroom's floral wallpaper and our giant Menudo poster.

The easier the words were to follow, the more I thrived on memorizing them. The simple lyrics in most Beatles tunes made them my absolute favorite. After devoting entire afternoons to this exercise, I could follow along whenever the songs played on the air! I felt like I belonged. I could do this for hours. Life simply went away when I practiced.

"Evelyn, hurry up, we're waiting!" Milady tapped me on the shoulder.

I took off the headset and rushed to the kitchen. Tío Edgardo, Tío Donel, Milady, and Daysi were already sitting around the brown kitchenette table, ready with paper and pencil. Time for our mandatory evening spelling bee. My uncles were on a crusade to help us master the language. I tried to visualize the words on the yellow wallpaper across from me, but the busy design made that task difficult. Some words were more difficult to learn than others. They helped us pronounce the most difficult English sounds, the ones that do not exist in Spanish.

Through.

World.

Storm.

Girl.

"Bit" not "beat."

"John" not "yawn."

"Winner" not "wiener."

"State" not "estate."

My uncles addressed us only in English and pretended not to understand us unless we did the same. No Spanish TV or Spanish radio or Spanish reading. At least not while my parents were at work, while they watched over us. They were merciless in making us answer the telephone despite our whining. The yellow phone terrified me. I never knew if the caller would understand Spanish. Their persistence eventually paid off.

We splashed right into our first summer by moving into the swimming pool of our apartment building. We had to be reminded to come inside to eat once in a while. My parents often had to forcibly remove our wrinkled bodies from the pool steps at night. We made friends with the other kids in the building who joined us in our daily routine of water games, helping the sunny Valley days go even faster.

I had not enjoyed myself this much since our family trips to *Los Chorros*, the water park just outside

San Salvador where my father taught us to swim. The surrounding forest and waterfalls that punched through rock enclosed the chilly pools at Los Chorros. The main pool was shallow enough for Papi to walk across to the island in the middle, but it was an abyss to my sisters and me. He "carried" us across the water with his arms stretched out as we paddled frantically with our skinny limbs and splattered a storm in his face. In our crazy commotion he lowered his arms into the water until we propelled ourselves across the water on our own.

When that first scorching summer came in the San Fernando Valley, we did not have to wait for sporadic outings to enjoy the water. We could practically smell the chlorine from the living room window of our apartment.

•   •   •

Just a few blocks from our apartment, Daysi adjusted on her own to life at Limerick Elementary School. She shared with us her common grade-school experiences — the ones that we missed out on, that everyone else seems to remember fondly: tether ball, kick ball, dodge ball, sock ball, reading groups, and a single classroom with a single teacher. But we still got plenty of our own at Columbus Junior High.

Sonia's life, on the other hand, was a whole world away. Despite her ambition and academic talent, Sonia's age confined her to a job as a live-in housekeeper to start. An honest living, but work that is physically and emotionally taxing, which some are never quite able to abandon. As we learned from Mami's years in it, its rewards often fall short.

Sonia began working shortly after New Year's Day, 1982. Tía Betty had found her a job as a live-in housekeeper with a Peruvian family in Cerritos, sixty miles south of our Valley apartment. She was hired to clean the house and watch the family's children. Like Mami's own domestic jobs over the years, Sonia's residence status was never questioned. The family had three boys, ages five, seven, and nine. Their exorbitant energy along with their mother's attitude made the job extremely demanding. Although the mother spoke Spanish, she never connected with Sonia on a personal or cultural level. Sonia's employer was caught up in the sense of "status" that their limited wealth had allegedly earned them. The physical demands of the job were exhausting. Personality quirks made it unbearable.

After her busy days, she spent her evenings in a small bedroom near the back of the two-story house. The bedroom window had a view of the garden in the backyard, but she seldom looked outside at night. On weekends she came home to us. Without a car, Sonia relied on my father to pick her up in our "new" orange Hornet station wagon. For the endless six months of her stay, she came home on Friday nights holding her sixty-dollar paycheck. She tried to recover her strength before Papi took her back for another week.

About the same time that we finished our first junior high school semester, Sonia got her next housekeeper job at a Beverly Hills home, a bit closer to us. She would replace Tía Betty, who was leaving for

El Salvador and wished to train Sonia to leave her in her place. The home belonged to an older couple with no children. More money, less stress.

At the end of her first day, Sonia let her hair down, changed out of her white uniform, and sat on the bed to watch TV in her windowless bedroom. Like Mami in her many years as a live-in, my sister did not get much time to herself in the daylight hours. Sadly, there was not much to do at night. The sparkling swimming pool in the backyard was off limits. This house was relatively smaller than the one before, three bedrooms, two baths, living room, family room, kitchen, and Sonia's quarters. The living room's white carpet and furniture made her job a lot more demanding than any other color would have. The countless crystal glasses hanging from racks above the bar took an entire morning to clean whenever the time came.

Her employers were kind, but they spoke no Spanish. Communicating with them was a daily struggle since at this time, Sonia could understand a whole lot more English than she could verbalize. They encouraged my sister to attend night school for English courses at Beverly Hills High. She earned eighty dollars a week to cook, clean, and run errands for them at nearby stores. One day, a few months later, another woman came to the house and Sonia was asked to show her the ropes. This woman was also Latina, slightly older than my sister. She spoke English well and drove her own car. After training the new lady, Sonia was informed on a mid-December day that she was being replaced. Her lady employer had some supportive words for her, encouraging her to seek out other opportunities where she might live up to her potential. She assured her that housekeeping was not the most fitting line of work for my sister. This lady could not have been more right about Sonia. But she was still out of a job.

Hoping to break a cycle before it was too late, Sonia's next housekeeper job was not a live-in position. The job was only a short bus ride away from our apartment. She took care of a three-year-old girl, who turned out to be key in refining Sonia's English skills. Sonia was treated like a part of the family. She attended night classes at Reseda High where she mastered the most advanced English-as-a-Second-Language levels and made lots of friends. Sonia worked for this Reseda family until early 1984, when financial problems forced them to cut her one-hundred twenty-dollar paycheck from their weekly budget. Sonia had to find a new job. She was immediately recommended for an interview at a nearby electronics company by one of her night-school friends.

At twenty years old, Sonia had never been through a job interview in her life. She was honest and eager.

"So, Sonia — do you know anything about electronics?

"No," she hesitated, "but I learn very fast.

"Do you have any transportation problems?

"No, no problem.

"Do you have any babysitter arrangements? You have kids, right?

She hesitated for a moment, but quickly answered that she had no children. What did babysitters have to do with this job?

"Why should we give you this job?

"I need the job, I want the job."

Blank stare.

"I want to learn, and I am ready to start," she added.

And that she did; she began her new position as an electronic board assembly inspector the following week, earning minimum wage, three dollars and twenty-five cents an hour. She worked on various assignments in different departments of this company. She received raises and promotions over the next six and a half years. She attended night school all of that time. Despite seeing her at home every weekend at first and most evenings eventually, Daysi, Milady, and I lived our parallel student days quite oblivious to Sonia's struggles and unaware of our own blessings.

•   •   •

Soon enough, our summer days in the pool were over and I was back to the routine of junior high school. Enter Roxana, a soft-spoken girl I met in Mr. Gherardi's eighth grade English class. Her family had moved to L.A. from Mexico when she was eight years old. Her family was very much like mine, hard working and humble, no fancy clothes or flashy shoes. They lived in a small apartment, much like ours. She had two sisters, one older and one younger. Their family rules were not as strict as ours, but we still did not hang out together much outside of school. She was shy and wore glasses as big as mine. She loved the *Menudo* lead singer more than I did, which was truly rare... She was practically my mirror image. We became inseparable.

We wrote to each other at least twice a day in our junior high school days. We wrote about music, hairstyles, soap operas, and campus gossip. Mostly, we wrote about boys — our crushes and our break-ups. We had an elaborate system of communication. We wrote in English or Spanish, depending on the topic. We nicknamed all our friends in a secret code, in case our letters fell into enemy hands. We held an unspoken pact of secrecy, our code never to be divulged to the prying masses. Written between every line, my plummeting self-esteem revealed itself.

Mr. Charles Gherardi made eighth grade English even harder than my first P.E. class the year before. His tortoise-shell glasses and graying beard framed a deep voice that rumbled through his classroom with authority. He had the highest expectations for his students but his mean reputation was a myth. He was as patient as he was kind. He had a gift for turning the torture of dictations, speeches, and role-plays into real learning experiences. In his ESL class, he regarded a heavy accent as a reminder of our ability to speak two languages rather than our imperfection in one of them.

Still, I often became nervous and froze. I would have been fine if I had a piece of paper to write it down first, but Mr. Gherardi showed me that I did not need a crutch. If I got stuck mid-sentence, he asked short questions to help me put my thoughts together. If I got stuck on a word, he recruited the class to help me along. He knew how self-conscious I was of my accent, yet Mr. Gherardi continued to call on me until the sound of my voice no longer felt strange.

He pushed each of us just outside our comfort zone to show us our on potential. Then, he gave me the big push at the end of eighth grade. He recommended that I transfer to "regular" English classes, leaving my sister Milady and my new friend Roxana spinning in the ESL cycle.

It became difficult for Roxana and me to talk about our future. My move to the "mainstream" English courses severed the few ties that she and I had. I was too new to be accepted by the overachievers, too removed to fit in with my Spanish-haven friends, and far too homely to hang with the "cool" club. I became a loner. Even my sisters called me boring. On the occasional Saturday night when my parents gave us permission to go out, I preferred homework to parties, to avoid the torture of not being asked to dance. No one accepted me.

•   •   •

The Mock Trial in my ninth grade Youth-and-Justice class slapped me right into the reality of life in "regular" English classes.

After much debate in class, I was selected to act as the prosecuting attorney, for which I had eagerly volunteered. I was excited about being such an important player in our project. I was asked to prosecute a man accused of beating his wife and children. I studied our brief textbook chapter on courtroom procedure and watched court television programs day in and day out to prepare. Never did it occur to me to ask my teacher for more reliable sources. Nevertheless, the day came and I felt ready. I dressed up in an old tweed suit and high-heeled pumps I snuck out of Mom's closet for the occasion. My oversized gray eyeglasses and limp hair parted on the left completed the nerdy seventies look. I was so excited that I hardly noticed the smelly containers of roofing asphalt my school was using for repairs near our bungalow. My heart pounded away with excitement when the bell rang for class.

I presented my case and questioned the first witness, the "wife," with skill and precision. I was quite pleased with my performance. As the defense attorney cross-examined my witness, things took a turn for the worse.

"So, Mrs. Jones, I understand you have a history of lying about your husband... Isn't it true that you have reported that your husband hit you in the past, only to take it back later?"
"Yes, but..."

"And isn't it true that all those times you lied about the violence in your home, you got lots of attention from your friends and family, and even the court?"

"Well, yes, but..."

My "client" begged me with her eyes to intercede. What was that word? It starts with an "o"...

"Well, maybe you just wanted some attention this time too, isn't that right?"

My rival was completely out of order. It was my place to say something. What <u>was</u> that word?

I could not remember it for the life of me: objection, objection, objection!   I beat my head over with that word for weeks after that, but it did not come to me when I needed it.   He went on and on.   My face burned with shame.   If my tears had escaped, they might have sizzled right off my cheeks

I thought if I stood up, it might come to me.

"Your Honor..." I started, silencing the room.

They all waited at the edge of their seats but I could not finish with the correct term.   Embarrassed by my obvious silence, others in the class tried to whisper the word to me to help me out.   But, not being quite adept at lip reading, I could not make out what they were saying.   I wanted to crawl under the building and die.   Better yet, I wanted to dive into one of the tubs of hot asphalt outside, to melt myself out of existence.   My opponent finally relented.   After that first witness stepped down, my nerves made me stumble on every word.   My first question for the second witness, the oldest child of the "accused":

"When were you were first *bitten* by your father?"

I realized my blunder halfway through my thought, as I visualized the correct spelling of every perfect sentence in my head.   "Beat", not "bit"! I had practiced this very word with my uncles at home countless times.   I knew the seriousness of my mistake long before the first burst of laughter, and tried to correct myself, but it was too late.   I might have run out of the room had it not been for my teacher.   Ms. Lee rescued me by cutting the diversion short.   She reminded our "judge" that a question had been asked that needed answering. I had actually volunteered for this torment. The trial ended soon enough. I won, I think, but it took me a while to get over the nasty mock trial episode.

The smell of roofing tar still brings back the sting of rejection from my first days out of ESL.

After years of struggling to overcome the heaviest of accents, my first honors class ever was tenth grade English at Canoga Park High. It was the Fall of 1984.

In class, I was on my own. Everyone else in that English class had been tracked into college-prep courses since grade school. Their circles were impenetrable by the time I worked my way in. At first, I was afraid and nervous to the verge of paranoia. I was afraid of being alone in a room full of people who knew each other well. None of my friends from Columbus had followed quite the same path. When reunited with my friends at lunchtime, there simply was not much in common anymore. We hardly had a word to say. Outside of class, I was even more alone.

Our social life was limited mostly to family functions and whatever interaction we could squeeze in between classes at school. We could always count on another of our aunts' friends to throw a house party on a Saturday night. Somehow, dancing cumbias takes on a different feel when you have your mother next to you on the dance floor. We did learn to value the times we could go out, even to visit with relatives, though. Going out presented a danger that my sisters and I could not begin to comprehend. These social restrictions were only partly driven by the traditional protective instincts that having four daughters instilled in my parents. They tried to explain the threats but I never quite understood the extent of their worry.

In El Salvador, the threats stared us directly in the face every day. When Archbishop Oscar Romero was assassinated in March of 1980, my sisters and I begged Papi to let us attend his memorial service and funeral. He gave us permission, but changed his mind at the last minute. Instead, we watched the ceremonies on TV. Multitudes turned out to catch a glimpse of the fallen leader. We watched in horror as shots were fired into the moving crowds from the roof of the Presidential Palace. The masses scattered but there was nowhere to run. We did not question our parents' concerns too much after that.

The threats became subtler once we left our country. The stability of our new lives was at anyone's mercy. If we were disliked, if any remark we made was misinterpreted as an insult, if employers, neighbors, or strangers suspected our legal status, we ran the constant risk of being reported to Immigration and deported. This could be done by anyone, for any reason. Our parents were determined not to let this happen. They limited our exposure to this threat, by not allowing us to socialize with our classmates after school, on weekends, or any time. My sisters and I were under the strictest of instructions not to reveal our status or even discuss our legal situation with anyone, regardless of how close a friend it might be.

In an apartment not too far away, Roxana, the closest of my Junior High friends, received the same instructions from her parents. We had written hundreds of letters to each other since the eighth grade, revealing the most intimate of secrets, but never once discussed the fact that we were both undocumented.

Our parents had to take the safe route; our lives were ruled by fear. This became tougher and tougher for my sisters and me to keep in mind as our teenage years went by.

•   •   •

Mrs. Anna Cohen was my eleventh grade chemistry teacher.   She was a rare gem — a brilliant, meticulous, creative, caring teacher.   The periodic table, endothermic reactions, chemical equilibrium, Vander Waals bonds, and LeChatelier's Principle made sense in Cohen-speak.   She was the only person capable of making these most heinous of topics even remotely bearable. And of convincing me that college was not as far-fetched a notion as I believed.

Mrs. Cohen always asked the most opportune questions at the most opportune times. One day, she asked me to stay after class to help her dismantle some lab equipment during lunch.

"So, you don't think you'll be applying to college?"

I shook my head.   She put down her tray of beakers and crucibles, rested her eyeglasses on her forehead like she always did, and frowned at me.

"And why not?"

"I don't think my parents can afford it."

Not a good enough reason, she said. Lots of help for low-income families, she said. I could not tell her the truth about our legal situation. She did not let up.

"I want you to ask your parents' permission to come to the Science Fair at USC next Saturday."

"But..."

"No buts! You tell them I said it's a class assignment, that you have to go, and they have to sign this form."

•   •   •

I had never before set foot on a college campus until the 1986 Science Fair at USC. I was enthralled by what I witnessed that day but I downplayed my excitement when I got home. I could never bring myself to torture my parents with the question of my education and my sisters', being so far beyond our financial and legal reach. I agonized over the thought of returning to chemistry class on Monday. How would I convince my teacher that I was not completely fascinated? Of course, Mrs. Cohen saw right through me and her persistence only grew, despite my pessimism.

Mrs. Cohen was finishing up the titration experiment she started in class when the bell rang and my classmates started filing out. She was wearing the same white coat and goggles that the USC technicians wore at the laser lab the Saturday before. She was concentrating through her bifocals, adding a chemical drop by drop into the tube of solution in front of her. I thought I could sneak out without talking about the Science Fair.

"Hold it!" she said as I passed by her counter, "help me rinse those beakers over there. Please."

Without taking her eyes off her experiment, she continued to put me on the spot.

"You liked the lasers... your eyes never lie!" she taunted me. I could not hide my smile.

I did not want to talk about it. I put some beakers into the sink and started to rinse them out.

"You can do this, Evelyn. College was made for you."

She placed a college application in my hand and harassed me until I filled it out.

Just a few weeks before my UCLA application was due that November, my parents filed applications for the six of us to become permanent U.S. residents under the Immigration Reform and Control Act of 1986. This legislation was the blessing my parents had prayed for all those years. In my family's case, this legalization process would ultimately bring the end of our life of silence and fear, but it took over three years and thousands of dollars to complete. Having so much riding on the applications, most people including my parents entrusted them to notary publics, lawyers, and preparers who greedily cashed in on the growing demand. They charged outrageous fees, with little oversight or accountability. My parents spent over $500 for each of us to be processed, including the preparer's fee, application charge, and costs for fingerprints, photographs, notarized letters, and physical exams.

We waited for hours at the packed clinic for our physical exams. We waited longer at that Koreatown clinic than at Children's Hospital in San Salvador, where the waits were practically sleepovers. This change in our status offered a glimmer of hope for our future. But there was no hope for a college education. My parents' combined income was less than the cost of college tuition each year. I had no one to lend me guidance or advice. No one in my family had ever attended a university in the U.S.

One November evening, I set up shop at the foot of the living room sofa, under the floor lamp, with a clipboard and the stack of forms that Mrs. Cohen had shoved in my hand. Admissions application, financial aid packet, scholarship forms... so many papers. I was still up to my neck in paperwork when Mami walked in from work.

"Mami, I need $35."

"$35? What for?"

"My teacher, Mrs. Cohen, says I should apply to a university. I have to send in the application next week. That's how much it costs."

"We'll get it for you, don't worry." She was beaming.

"Mami, one more thing... the application is asking me if I am a California permanent resident or a non-resident." She instantly stopped beaming.

"Really?" she blurted.

"What do you think I should say?"

Her eyes glazed over with worry and her lips did not move.

"Well, if I say I'm a 'permanent resident', would they call Immigration to find out if it's true?"

"No se, hija."

"Well, what if I get the whole family in trouble?"

"We'll just have to take that risk."

"Really, Mami?"

She smiled again.

The most straightforward question on the entire form became the most difficult to answer. The application, in fact, only asked about "residence" to determine whether to charge out-of-state tuition fees. Nothing related to immigration. I had lived in California for over one year and qualified but did not know it. The risk to my family was too great. So, naturally, I left the question blank and hoped that no one would notice. I finished my essay on the last possible day. My parents scraped together the money I needed and I mailed the package in with a prayer. If I had known about application fee waivers for low-income students, I might have applied to more than one campus. But with no information beyond Mrs. Cohen's coaching, I applied to a single school: UCLA. I was determined not to get my hopes up.

All my classmates' college acceptance letters had been received, read, and celebrated for weeks. Maybe mine was delayed because of our move to San Fernando; to the house my parents bought that February. If they responded in the order the applications were received, I would be lucky to get any response at all. Or perhaps the admissions committee was still laughing at my essay, passing it around for kicks.

I was at home when my father brought the mail in that afternoon. He walked in the door holding out the envelope, recognizing the blue and gold UCLA logo on the return address. I could not take it from him. Instead I took his hand and squeezed it, trying to transfer some of his strength to me. His hand was still as warm and strong and gentle as it had always been, although no longer three times the size of mine. I finally took the letter and Papi put his arm around me. We stared at the envelope for a minute. If it had been any thinner, it would have been empty.

Which envelope brings good news? Thick or thin?

The rims of my eyes were flooded with anticipation. I took a deep breath, turned it over, ripped it open, and read the first word.

"Congratulations!"

We hugged and cried and jumped and cried some more. Five years, two months, and three weeks after leaving El Salvador, I was accepted into UCLA's entering class of 1987.

MARCHES

Move-in day: the last Monday of June 1987.

I had anxiously awaited the beginning of the UCLA Freshman Summer Program for over two months, my parents an entire lifetime. Two weeks after my graduation from Canoga Park High, Mom and Dad drove me to campus in our station wagon, filled to the brim with my things. Papi double-parked the orange Hornet in the congested cul-de-sac in front of Sproul Hall. We stacked my stuff onto a tiny spot on the sidewalk. He shouted over the rowdy conversations around us that he would be back to get me on Friday afternoon. He did that with religious punctuality for the next seven weeks. He hugged me good-bye and turned the car around to go to work.

Mami and I made a few trips to my sixth floor room to carry everything up. My roommate had not yet made it in, so I chose the bed on the left. It only took a few minutes for Mami and me to set my things in place. The room still looked barren when we were done. My mom gave me $40 that she could not afford and told me to call home every day. She had a million things to say, but didn't. A few awkward moments later, Mami and I said good-bye. I walked her downstairs, gave her a tight hug, and watched her walk away to take the bus home.

I skipped the crowds at the elevator and raced back up the six flights of stairs to my room, grinning from ear to ear, closed the door and did a little dance. My own room, thirty miles away from home... away from the clutter, from my parents, from my sisters — for seven glorious weeks. I walked to the window and pulled the drapes open to let the sun stream in. George Michael's "I Want Your Sex" was blaring from a boom box propped against a window across the way. I let out a primal scream and laughed out loud. WOW. This was it – my own life. *Could this be real?*

Downstairs, Mami made her way through the maze of students and parents. They dashed in front of her carrying luggage, piles of clothes on hangers, crates of books and compact discs, and rolled-up U2 posters. She did not walk to the bus stop after all.

Instead, she wandered about campus alone, overwhelmed with a sadness she could not explain. She was unsure how to handle a loss that was not a loss in the least, a blessing that caused her so much grief. She was unsure how to feel about her child being torn from her, no matter the reason. She was afraid of the freedom I would have while I was away, afraid to let go while thankful for her chance to do so. With tears streaming down her face, she walked slowly through the same plazas, courtyards, and corridors that I passed by on my way to class during the next five years.

While I danced and laughed in my dorm room on the other side of campus, she marched aimlessly, thinking and crying in silence. Hours passed, in fact, before she ever caught the bus home.

The next morning, I walked into my very first college lecture. Pre-Calculus. The room sloped steeply down to the lecturer stage. I sat somewhere mid-way up, close enough to see clearly, far enough not to be picked on, at least that first day. There were at least one hundred and fifty students in the lecture hall. Accelerated high school math courses and summer school did not compensate for my late start in the "college prep" track. I only got as far as trigonometry at Canoga High. The Professor asked his first question.

"How many of you passed the Advanced Placement Calculus test in High School?"

Over half of the students raised their hands. This was Pre-Calculus and more than half of the class belonged in courses two levels above this one. I was in a different environment than I had ever been before. Every one of these students was used to being the brightest, the smartest, the best — and they had become my competition.

•   •   •

During the second week of summer school, someone passed me a handwritten note in Math class. It had jagged edges and was folded in half.

> *Info Meeting for*
> *Undocumented Students*
> <u>*Tonight*</u> *— See Joe for location*
> **(Pass it on)**

"What's this?"

My classmate said nothing. I looked up at Joe, our Math tutor, who was standing by the door with his arms crossed, wearing a black Ché Guevara t-shirt, and the distinctive braid that fell half way down his back. He nodded at me. I looked away immediately and passed the note to the person behind me. Did anyone notice that? At the end of class, I passed by Joe on my way out. Without a word or even eye contact, he handed me a small piece of paper.

Sproul 423   7pm

I took it from him, also without a word.

At a quarter to seven, I paced around my dorm room, annoying my roommate as she tried to finish some homework. It must be some joke. I wondered if anyone would be stupid enough to set up a meeting like that, let alone show up for it. My parents would KILL me if they knew I went to something like this. Still, I had <u>so</u> many questions. Would there ever be a chance for me to ask anyone about being an undocumented student? What did that residence question mean on the application form? What about financial aid? Who could I trust? Better go check it out. If anything looked suspicious, I could make up an excuse and leave.

The door was cracked open, using a book as a doorstop. A few whispers trickled out, voices blended together. The room was dimly lit. No signs on the door. But there wouldn't be. I knocked and started to push open the door when I heard Joe's familiar voice.

"Come on in, we'll get started in a few minutes."

I walked in looking straight down, hoping not to recognize anyone, and most of all not to be recognized myself. A few people were huddled on futons on either side of the room. Legs dangled from the loft beds above us. A single lamp sat on the desk with a fringed orange scarf thrown over it. I found a spot against the wall next to a futon, where I sat resisting the urge to look around. The moment I looked up, I noticed Juan, Susie, and Mario from my Math class sitting right across from me. Juan pursed his lips together into an embarrassed smile. I recognized Carolina from my Computer science class, and a few other faces from around the dorm. I had thrown away my anonymity. Maybe no one would notice if I got up and left now.

"We know this may not be very comfortable for most of you," Joe started.

Too late to run now.

"We called this meeting because we know people need information that sometimes they can't ask for. We're not taking names. We just want to share some of what we know. Maybe then, you'll know where you can get answers to some of your questions."

Joe told us about the 1985 Leticia A. ruling, the California court decision that made it possible for me to attend a university despite my legal status. He discussed how filing a residence application through the Amnesty Program guaranteed in-state tuition fees. I could not know it at that time, but it would take my family three long years to complete the Amnesty process. During this time, as before, our lives could end up in someone else's hands if we were not careful. Joe talked about financial aid — what to ask, what to expect, worst case scenarios. I had earned several scholarships for academic excellence and need-based grants to pay entirely for my first year at UCLA. Joe reminded us that these funds were at risk too. Yes, we should expect vindictive people. Just like anywhere else - professors, fellow students, folks in the registrar's office, may be willing to phone Immigration to report us. Be discreet, Joe said. He did not allow us to ask questions. If we needed to know more, he advised us talk to him outside this meeting and to guard the details of our situation as closely as we could.

•   •   •

The two classes I took during the Freshman Summer Program gave me the foundation I needed to begin my studies in the fall with a perfect 4.0 grade point average. Plus, that first summer generated an interesting byproduct. I had grown smug. The first week of school put me, and my delusion of grandeur, to the test. Three days into the Fall quarter, I was called into the Financial Aid Office. One of the counselors was waiting for me, holding my file in her hand.

"I am confused," she confessed as she sat down, "you have left your residency question blank."

"Yes." It didn't go unnoticed. Despite Joe's clandestine advice that summer, I was deathly afraid to call myself a "resident" under any circumstance, fearing I'd be asked for proof and, as a result, incriminate my entire family.

"So, are you declaring yourself a California resident?"

"No." Her confusion grew.

"Wait, so, you are a non-resident?"

Be discreet, Joe had said. Could she be one of the vindictive ones? No way to know. I looked around her office for some sign that it was okay to trust her. Nothing. After a few moments of silence, she raised her eyebrows, prompting my reply.

"Yes."

"But you attended high school in California last year," she flipped to the front of the file, "at Canoga Park High?"

"Yes."

"That means you are a California resident," she insisted.

"But I am not a resident."

"That makes no sense. Is there something you're not telling me?"

She would not understand until I came clean about my legal status. Mami's voice echoed in my head: we will just have to take that risk. Here goes nothing.

"I mean," I whispered, leaning in, "I am not a *legal* resident yet."

She sat back in her chair. She understood everything.

"It's okay," she said. "You are eligible for a Cal-Grant to pay your tuition and I have your check right here. Look, from my desk, I have all the information I need to approve this right now. None of that other stuff has to do with tuition."

She could tell I was hesitant.

"What I mean is, for this purpose, you're a resident. You let us know when the rest of it is sorted out, okay?" she asked.

I nodded reluctantly.

She placed a "CALIFORNIA RESIDENT" stamp in my file. She handed me my first financial aid check and sent me on my way.

I walked out with my heart in my throat, with a check in my hand, and an hour free before my noon class. In a lapse of freshman wisdom, I decided that I had enough time to walk one mile into Westwood Village, cash my check at the bank, walk back to the bookstore, find all my textbooks and pay for them, and still leave plenty of time to get to my Geology Lab at twelve o'clock.

Miraculously, I made it back from the bank and through the cash-only line at the bookstore with 5 minutes to spare. The cashier fit the books for all my classes into two large yellow bags. The bags were made of that thick crinkly plastic that makes loud noises when it moves. They weighed about a thousand pounds each. I dragged the bags along the floor to push them out of the way.

I pulled out my wrinkled class schedule printout from my backpack and looked up the room for my two-hour Lab. I knew the campus like the back of my hand after the summer. "Math Science 5421." Easy. I even had a shortcut to get there.

I swung the door open at precisely twelve o'clock. Class had already begun. There were twenty older male students inside, all wearing glasses. The professor stopped talking and they all looked up in unison. If my bookstore bags hadn't been so loud, you could have heard a pin drop. There were Calculus graphs all over the board. Clearly, not my Geology Lab. I stepped away and let the door shut by itself. I pulled out that printout again. I had just raced to the room for my math class the next day.

Okay, so my actual room was in the Geology Building. Geology 3157. I was only a little late and I found the room right away. I put one of the bags down and opened the door, bringing the lecture to a halt. Every one of the fifty students was staring right at me. The professor had been talking for fifteen minutes already, so it was impossible to be undisruptive. I scanned the room as I walked in. The only empty seats were at the very back. The slower I walked, the louder my bags became. Half way in, I made a quick dash to the back, sat down, and let my bags thump onto the floor. Anything to make them stop staring. The professor resumed his talk. I took a deep breath and reached into the bag and pulled out my new Geology workbook in one loud crunch. I unzipped my backpack notch by notch and pulled out all my pens one by one. After five grueling, very loud minutes, I was ready and I looked up at the chalkboard. The professor's name was written across the top. Right below it, a room number. Geology 3425.

Oh, no.

Twice in one day — is that possible? Before I had time to think, I dumped everything back into the noisy bags and bolted out of the back door. I looked at the printout again to be sure. Geology 3157. I looked at the number on the door and back at the printout.

3. 1. 5. 7.

Door, printout. Door, printout.

It was the right room, all right. The number I'd seen on the board was the professor's office. It was 12:25 p.m. and I was in the hallway. Noisy bags and all. It was my first day in this Lab. I couldn't possibly miss it. I was ready to sneak back in through the back door, but it had no doorknobs. Of course. I made myself walk back in through the front door.

Every face in the room was frozen with disbelief and a single question hanging on their lips.

"Didn't you just do this ten minutes ago?"

By 12:30 p.m., I was settled into my back row seat again, ready to learn. Three short days into my college career, I had surpassed the humiliation of my Junior High Mock Trial. I had heard that most of the learning that happens in college takes place outside the classroom, but this was ridiculous. Back at the dorm, my friends could not believe I went back in. It never even occurred to me that I had any other choice.

This could be my only shot. I couldn't blow it.

Life shifted into high gear. Classes, tutorials, study groups, exams, meetings, aerobics classes, and new friends occupied my every moment. The months passed and I disappeared from my family. It was seven a.m. one morning when the phone startled my roommate and me awake. With my eyes still closed, I reached for the phone from under the covers.

"Hello..."

"Halo. Hija. Where were you last night?"

"Mami?"

"Where did you go? I called you, it was after 11 o'clock."

Here we go. It was too early to start with that.

"I was studying down the hall, Mom. We have a test today at nine."

"Are you coming home this weekend?"

"I want to Mom, but we have a test this Monday too."

"It's your Mama Lola's birthday, you know."

"I know. I really want to be there. Please tell her I love her. Okay?"

In the beginning, my father had shown up at my dorm every Friday to take me home, without even a phone call to confirm that I would be there. I was eighteen years old, but I did not dare make plans to be anywhere but the campus without calling to ask their permission first.

Deep down, I know they wanted to believe that I was not out living the wild life they suspected. Eventually, they trusted me to stay over the weekend to study without question. Soon enough, Mami stopped calling, not because she didn't want to or didn't care. It was her way of telling me she believed I was doing the right thing and that she trusted my judgement.

My family's lives went on without me. Each time I came home, I felt more removed from them. Soon enough, I felt like I had more in common with my Calculus study partners than with my own sisters. Once in a blue moon, I got to join them at a birthday party or a baby shower, where I got reacquainted with familiar faces and where I met an entire generation of cousins who were born while I was away.

•   •   •

My friend Charisse and I met that first summer at UCLA. We had grown up thousands of miles and worlds apart. I had shared a bedroom with my three sisters most of my life. As the single child of an engineer and a teacher, she always had her very own room. While I visited my family in the Salvadoran countryside, Charisse drove cross-country with her parents. As I learned to drop to the ground at the sound of an explosion, she played sports and sold cookies for the Girl Scouts. While I celebrated my *quinceañera* in a San Fernando Church, she attended a cotillion in her honor, hosted by her mother's Alpha Kappa Alpha sorority. Yet despite having such different childhoods, we shared very much the same adolescence.

Our first conversation was an argument over the solution to a trigonometry problem. We both sat in the front row.

"I don't think that's the right way to do it," I said, peeking rudely at her notebook.

"But I got the right answer!" she replied.

"Right, but this way is so much faster," I pointed proudly at my own solution.

She disagreed. Our discussion disrupted the class to the point that the professor asked us both to be quiet or step outside. We laughed a little and bonded instantly.

Troy and I met at Charisse's eighteenth birthday party. My future husband sat with patient ears through my most involved anecdotes about El Salvador and the war. He asked more questions about my past than anyone had ever asked me. We talked constantly for the first few months. I was eager to share more information, and Troy wanted to hear my opinions as well. Within the first month, I took Troy to meet my parents. I had never taken anyone home for them to meet. They immediately reinstated their old come-home-every-weekend requirement.

•   •   •

Every semester, as Troy and I studied for midterms together, we got sidetracked debating intense topics. War. Defense spending. The space program. And then, there was the big one, of course. Immigration. He never let me get away with answers like "I don't know" or "I never thought about that." He forced me to make up my mind, to defend my opinions, and taught me to agree to disagree. This was not an overnight process.

"Well, I know they are breaking the law," Troy replied to a question of mine. I responded with yet another question.

"But do you agree with the law that they are 'breaking'?"

"What do you mean?"

"Should you convict a person even if you disagree with the interpretation of the law?"

"Give me an example."

"A man steals medicine for his sick wife because he can't afford to pay for it — would you convict him?"

"Well, I could sympathize, but his action would still be illegal. I would have to convict him. I would probably consider his circumstances in sentencing."

"But he would be a criminal in your mind?"

"Yes. I would recommend some assistance programs for him or something."

"I can't believe you would consider him a petty criminal."

"All I'm saying is people need to go through the established process."

"People just like undocumented immigrants, you mean?"

"There should be some order to it. I never had a problem with immigration, just the illegal kind."

"Wow — I see."

"Don't you think there should be some controls, some sort of order to it?"

"Never mind."

It was hopeless. Troy was the person closest to me but I would never convince him that a piece of paper should never have so much weight. Discussing our views would only make them stronger for him and more frustrating for me.

"Please tell me," he insisted.

"I hear you telling me what my family did is wrong. That will always be hard for me to hear.

"That's not what I said. I'm not saying it was wrong, it just happens to be illegal.

"Do you think that they shouldn't be here, that they should all be sent back?

"I think each case should be weighed individually.

"But do you think they should all be deported?

"Well, they shouldn't be surprised if they're caught and deported as a result.

"So you don't think they should be here.

"That's not what I said.

"Never mind."

Somehow we always came back around to the flashcards we were meant to be studying, our opinions grew stronger, and all was well.

Troy and I often forgot how our different childhoods shaped us and continue to affect us every day, sometimes in the most obscure, bizarre ways. There were television shows, foods, games, music, and even commercial jingles that made him nostalgic about growing up in Los Angeles in the 1970s. It happened often as we flipped randomly through channels on the TV - often enough that it was obvious how much fun he had as a kid.

"I need to get 'SPEED RACER' on tape – I love that show. Do you remember that?"

"No, we didn't get that show in El Salvador.

"What did you guys watch?

"Wonder Woman, the Flintstones, the Six-Million Dollar Man, Mission Impossible, the Hulk...

"You watched the Hulk, in Spanish?

"Yeah, all the good shows were translated. You should listen to Barney Rubble's voice when it's translated to Spanish, it's high-pitched and totally opposite to what it should be. It messed me up.

"What about Saturday morning cartoons?

"We got those too, Bugs Bunny, Pink Panther, Casper, Popeye, George of the Jungle, Plastic Man, you name it, we got it. We would take the cash Papi left us for tortillas for lunch and spend it on cookies, muffins, and sodas at the corner store.

"For breakfast?", he sounded appalled.

"Like you never did it. It's not like I still eat like that. I'm getting a sugar rush just thinking about it.

"We should have something healthy for dinner tonight. How about seafood?," he suggested.

"Oh no, I don't eat fish," I replied with a disgusted look.

"Why not?

"I don't know, I just don't like it.

"When was the last time you had it?

"I don't remember.

"So how do you know you still don't like it?

"I don't see what the big deal is. You can have seafood, if you want. I'll just order chicken or something.

"Sounds like there's a good reason for that, though, I am just curious..."

Troy never gave up easily. I reluctantly nodded.

"So what's the reason?", he insisted.

I hadn't thought about this in years. We never ate fish in the years before moving to the U.S. for the goriest of reasons.

"You remember all the stories I told you about the war back in El Salvador? And all the people who disappeared and were found dead later? Many of them were found in rivers where fish and other animals could get to them. Many bodies were unrecognizable, missing parts, even before decomposition set in. Freshwater seafood was out of the question. We could never be sure of where the fish at the markets was coming from. Eventually the smell or even the thought of seafood grossed me out. So, I don't eat fish."

He was horrified.

"Sorry... you asked," I apologized.

It took a while even for Troy to be able to eat fish after that conversation. Years later, I was able to join him and enjoy seafood without thinking about my graphic reasons for hating it before.

•   •   •

Sophomore Year brought with it my first dreaded physics course. I had never taken Physics before, but the stories I'd heard made me shiver with fear. I found a seat in the middle of the lecture hall, so as to get lost amidst the two hundred other faces in the class. Then Professor Bengtsson entered, looking far too young to be any kind of Professor, wearing an outfit straight out of a Banana Republic catalog, a white button down shirt, khaki pants, tiny round John-Lennon eyeglasses, and a red bandana tied across his neck. His over-the-eye hairdo would have fit more in a Duran Duran video than in a theoretical physics class.

He gave us the most unusual welcome, with some remarks about his plans to instill a deep curiosity in each of us about, of course, physics. He said we'd be checking physics books from the library that were not required before he was done with us. Then he started to unbutton his shirt. He said that everything we saw, heard, and maybe even believed could be explained with physics concepts. His shirt was completely off by this time. The entire class had to pick their jaw up off the floor.

We would learn to question everything we saw, he said. He continued to talk as he slipped off his Birkenstock sandals and started to undo his pants. His teaching assistants brought out a bed of nails, and by the time they placed on the demo counter, our young professor had stripped down to his blue Speedos. He took an apple and threw it up in the air directly over the razor-sharp nails, piercing halfway through the apple when it landed. He smiled as he took the fruit out and took a bite. There are no tricks, he said. Physics would explain it all. He lay down on the bed of nails. Before we knew it, his teaching assistants had placed two slabs of concrete on his chest and smashed them with a sledgehammer. He didn't flinch.

Our interest peaked, indeed. By the end of the term, he had shattered roses dipped in liquid nitrogen and walked across hot coals, and wrote test questions that read more like short stories than physics problems.

"If you take a cat, you turn him upside down, and let him drop, he will always land on all fours. Why?"

What kind of professor asks this on a physics midterm? Professor Bengtsson did. After his class, I locked in my decision to study Civil Engineering. The prestige carried by the title of "Engineer" is unsurpassed in my country and my family's minds. The pride in my parents' faces when I announced my choice was reason enough to do it. After two enlightening years, I applied to the Civil Engineering Department and was accepted.

•   •   •

I rushed into Campbell Hall, home of the Tutorial Lab where I worked as a Pre-Calculus tutor my second and third years. It paid twelve dollars an hour, as much as my sister Sonia earned in one day as a live-in not too long before. This was one of the highest-paying student jobs on campus, but that was only part of why I loved working there as much as I did. The lab was part of the Academic Advancement Program, the same program that brought hundreds of first-generation and underrepresented students to study on campus their first summer — the same program where I learned Pre-Calculus in the first place. In a way, this was a chance to give back some of what they had given me.

I was early that morning, a whole five minutes to spare before my nine o'clock Pre-Calculus tutoring session. The entire hallway was lined with blue flyers.

<u>DEMAND MORE SPACE</u>
FOR THE
AAP TUTORING LAB!!!!

RALLY TODAY

FRIDAY 11/16/90
NOON
CAMPBELL HALL STEPS

It was my 21st birthday. I couldn't think of a better way to celebrate. Ever since my family and I received our permanent residence cards the year before, I had found a voice I didn't know I had. I spotted Alicia, the History tutor who organized the rally, posting flyers at the very end of the hall. We did need the space. Tutors were forced to out shout each other, with groups of students crammed into small rooms. We had been fined by the Fire Department for tutoring in the hallways. Most of the tutors were convinced that more space would be allocated if the program didn't focus on helping minority students. My belligerence only grew when I began to look around in my science lecture halls. I found myself, as a woman and as a Latina, alone. I knew that this imbalance did not represent our potential. The only programs that seemed to be helping these students were sorely under resourced and ignored by the administration.

I ran to meet Alicia and offered to help make signs after my tutoring sessions. She asked me to speak at the rally and I agreed. In my impromptu speech, I attacked the UCLA Chancellor directly, pointing at his posh office in Murphy Hall. Chancellor Charles Young had spent the better part of the past year spouting stories about his commitment to diversity.

"If you are so dedicated to diversity, Mr. Charles, Young, why don't you show us *and not tell us what your commitment is?"*

A campus photographer snapped a photo of Alicia and me leading the march to the Administration Building. I carried one of the signs I helped to make.

"Hey, Chuck, can we tutor in your *hallway?"*

That one was my favorites. My parents would have had heart attacks if they knew that photo made the front page of the Daily Bruin.

We marched with one hundred tutors and students directly into Chancellor Young's office, where we found out he was gone for the day. Of course. As we walked out of the building, I looked at my watch and gasped. I tossed my sign to Alicia and started to run across campus. I had five minutes to get to my structural engineering midterm.

•   •   •

Two quarters later, that same school year, I sat at the poorly lit desk in my dorm room, fuming. Again. I plowed through page after page of scratch paper, scribbling out my thoughts on the 1990 Bradford decision. This Superior Court decision overturned the Leticia A. Ruling, allowing campuses to deny financial aid to students based on legal status and charge out-of-state tuition to undocumented students, who are often from the neediest families. I wrote about my childhood, about growing up amidst a war that had nothing to do with me, describing the reluctant silence that ruled our lives for so long. I wrote about the war being waged against undocumented students, whose only "crime" was lacking a piece of government-issued paper. A war waged against a people who cannot speak up, much less fight back.

I circled around my tiny room, throwing my arms around, rushing to my desk to jot my next lines. I pointedly accused the UCLA administration of covering up critical information.   Gone were the days of clandestine meetings in darkened dorm rooms to discuss the issue. I confessed my family's truth to the world. The campus no longer had to wonder what an "illegal alien" looks like. It looks like me.

My anger had taken over.

I was no longer concerned with fact. I accused the administration of agreeing with Bradford's ultimate plan to shut out students despite their dedication or their ability, based strictly on their possession of a "green card." I thought of Julio, an undocumented freshman I had recently met. He was real, not some statistic, not some application form without a face. Julio's soft-spoken nature was born from fear and not from a lack of opinion. His hopes, aspirations, and the dreams of an entire family hung by a thread. Julio's future did not depend on his academic brilliance or commitment.   It depended on the loudness of the voices of those with the freedom to speak. The law that Bradford overturned had protected me. It was Julio's turn. I was the only voice he had.

I stayed up half the night to finish. My temples radiated with the beginning of a headache that would linger for at least a week. I plopped down on the bed and fell asleep knowing the school paper would never print my letter.   I was very surprised when it was published the same week, unaltered. A Daily Bruin reporter contacted me to discuss the cover-up mentioned in my letter. We found that there was no such cover-up, only internal memos on the status of their ongoing litigation with Bradford. I had put the spotlight on a topic in hopes that fairness would prevail.

After my letter was published, I received many sideways and puzzled looks from my classmates. They were stunned by the facts the paper revealed. My parents, too, were baffled by my willingness to disclose what they might call our embarrassing truth. They struggled to accept my habit of challenging authority. It was difficult for them to distinguish what I was doing on campus from the political rallies back home during the war. After watching guerrilleros take over my elementary school all those years back, my thirst for political involvement should have surprised me too.

I was a self-proclaimed symbol, a champion for the underdog in my community. I was living proof that the stereotypes clinging to me, waiting outside my door, were figments of the collective imagination and nothing more. I was out to disprove the bogus image of the welfare-bound, self-serving, non-English-speaking, job-stealing illegal alien, and, of course, of the non-thinking, high-heel-wearing, P-M-S-ing, tantrum-throwing, cat-fighting, my-nail-broke-whining, helpless woman. I was sick and tired of being labeled and I was convinced the whole world needed a wake up call.

After two more years of campus jobs, and academic hurdles, I found myself sitting, pen in hand, on the steps of a UCLA quad. I stared at the manicured lawn, at the mosaic of freshly planted geraniums, enjoying the lingering notes spilling out of the Music Building. My mother had marched through this very quad five years before, crying, as I celebrated my arrival on the other side of campus. In a few days, I would stand on a stage in Pauley Pavilion, before my graduating class, my engineering professors, plus three thousand friends and family members, to deliver the speech of my life. I scribbled in a notebook a few final thoughts for my speech. How did I get here?

Ten years had passed since I bid farewell to the Duralita rooftops of my sleeping neighborhood, ten years since that sliver of December sky, framed by barren trees and renewed promise, greeted my young eyes to a new country and a new life. Thirteen years had passed since a fateful storm on a humid afternoon introduced me to miracles and guardian angels. Even longer, since I longed for my mother as I blew out birthday candles and showed off my American clothes and toys to jealous neighbors and friends. I relived for a second, the torment of my P.E. classes in the Valley, and the humiliation of the Mock Trial that killed my self-esteem. My upcoming speech seemed even more like a dream. I thought of my sister Sonia, only six years older than I, a victim of timing, slated away from school for being "too old"... I realized that she had to put in ten times the effort to get out of that cycle, studying on her own at night while struggling during the day, elbow-deep in Windex and running after spoiled brats of the well-to-do. She had lived a life so removed from mine. I thought of my mom selling *pan dulce* as a girl, of my dad picking cotton in the sun-scorched fields of Usulután. I wanted a speech that would make them proud.

Still, I needed a speech that would pull in every person in the audience. I thought back just two years before, to the anti-war rallies that gripped the campus during Desert Storm. I thought of my students' faces and how they lit up when they got the right answer during a tutoring session. I thought of the marches to protest the UC tuition hike that quadrupled fees during my five-year stay. I thought of the Los Angeles police officers who beat Rodney King and were acquitted just two months before. I thought of the riots that ensued, gripping the city. I had to come up with a way to discuss the riots in my speech.

My fellow graduates expected a light-hearted address, something humorous to take away on their last day on campus. A classmate greeted me moments before the ceremony,

"Just make it funny, okay?" she said in passing.

I was set out to disappoint her. The speaker selection committee before whom I auditioned had not been interested in "funny." They had selected my speech with a theme of social responsibility in the engineering profession. The committee members sat behind me on the Pauley Pavilion stage as I stepped to the podium. My political statements took them by surprise. I discussed the most overwhelming challenge for engineering professionals, the challenge of awareness in a society still fostering institutionalized oppression. I reminded them of the burning L.A. skyline that each of us witnessed just weeks before, of the angry energy produced by that oppression. I could hear the right-wing Republicans squirming in their seats.

I had done my job.

After graduation, I had no idea how much I had yet to learn about the politics of work. Being part of the "minority" in college only gave me a glimpse of what was to come. I was younger, darker, and a different gender than most engineers with whom I would interact over the next few years.

But that is a whole other story.

•   •   •

In 1994, a full five years after receiving our permanent residence cards, my entire family and I became eligible for U.S. citizenship. Ever since my protesting days in school, I longed for the ability to raise my political voice through my vote. I filed as soon as I could get my application completed early that summer. But the next major election would come before I could become naturalized. It was the most frustrating political exercise I have ever consciously and purposely taken part in.

The California gubernatorial elections were exactly three weeks away. I joined a phone campaign to educate voters about the ramifications of a "reasonable" suspicion clause in Proposition 187. If it passed, the Proposition would deny social services, health care, and education to anyone suspected of being an undocumented immigrant. If it passed, teachers might have to report students to the INS. By law, doctors would have to report their patients, social workers their clients, police officers their law-abiding citizens. "Reasonable suspicion" was enough. People like me would remain "reasonably suspicious" as long as we had the same complexion, the same dark eyes, the same slight accent, the same Spanish surname.

The Proposition found its strongest supporter at the top of California's State government, with Governor Pete Wilson. Wilson's own re-election campaign fed on the general immigrant "scare" which invariably surfaces every election year and at times of financial crisis.

I posed questions to anyone who would listen. How many people would refuse to report crimes or visit hospitals or send their children to school from fear of being deported? How many immigrants would be discriminated against due to the color of their skin? How many blonde, blue-eyed "suspects" would be questioned about their legal status?

A march was organized in East Los Angeles to protest Prop 187. A few Spanish radio stations had announced it every day for a couple of weeks. My sister Daysi was eager to come and bring my three-year old nephew, Alex. When we arrived, we put the baby in the stroller and walked past vast crowds of people at each corner passing out signs. We took a couple of signs: one declared *"Los Indocumentados Pagan Impuestos"* ("The Undocumented Pay Taxes") and the other said *"No a la 187."* I gave my nephew a whistle shaped like a soccer ball so he could also join in. As we approached the corner of Lorena Avenue and recently-renamed Cesar Chavez Boulevard, I realized immediately that the attendance forecasts had been far too conservative. We were an hour early and already there were people lined up as far as the eye could see.

Hundreds of people walked around with signs and T-shirts opposing the Proposition. Several crews of

Brown Berets, seasoned by decades of systematic protests, rallies, marches, and walkouts, directed the crowds with precision.

People lined up from the south corner of Lorena facing Chavez Boulevard, in groups: Labor unions, community groups, high schools, university clubs, educators, religious groups, health care providers, and concerned citizens like my sister and me. We found our place near the front of the growing masses, just a couple of hundred yards behind the March's leaders.

People brought their children, their parents, their friends, their classmates, their co-workers, their neighbors, and their pets. As ten o'clock drew near, I looked back behind us, down Lorena Avenue. I could no longer see the end of the crowd. The loudness of the conversations around us blared in my ears and brought a smile to my face. I gave my sign to little Alex as he sat in his stroller, and I walked down the street. My heart raced with every step, as I tried to look up over the top of the crowd. I rejoiced at the infinite sea of people, signs floating above their heads, filling block after block after block, gathering across intersections. On that sunny Sunday, over one hundred thousand people flocked to East Los Angeles to march over the L.A. River Bridges to City Hall. A harmony of familiar chants echoed on the boulevard.

"EL PUEBLO — UNIDO — JAMAS SERA VENCIDO!"

"THE PEOPLE — UNITED — WILL NEVER BE DEFEATED!"

The turnout exceeded anyone's wildest expectations. News helicopters hovered above us recording the event for their six o'clock weekend reports. The crowd of activists over one mile long traveled the five-mile march route. Countless observers stood on every sidewalk along the way, lining the nearby streets, cheering from every corner, looking from every store window, peering from every door. Curious faces welcomed the familiar sight of their national flags: Mexico's red, white, and green. The various blue and white flags of Central America also showed up in numbers: Guatemala, El Salvador, Nicaragua, Honduras, and Costa Rica, each raised with pride. Bystanders cheered for their own countries, their own children, their own faces on parade.

Many older, first generation immigrants often objected to political activities, yet they showed up in force. For many, identifying with political causes has turned people into living targets. Some of these people chose to stay home and cheer silently from their living room television sets. Others chose to look from their windows above Chavez Boulevard.

As we marched on, I found myself floating in the crowd through a dark tunnel just half a mile from City Hall. The tunnel was only a couple of city blocks, but the multitude squeezing through its narrow lanes made it stretch for miles. The arched tunnel walls forcibly bounced back our chants and shouts, magnifying them tenfold. The tiny light at the tunnel's end was fixed in space as we slowly worked our way to it. With the loudness reaching dizzying levels, and our pupils still adjusting to the darkness of our path, it was difficult to know which direction was forward or even which way was up.

We flowed miraculously through the cramped space with scarcely more than standing room, moved by the force of our conviction and excitement. Slightly worried about my nephew's take on the commotion, I put my hand on the stroller for balance and bent down to look at him, squinting to focus in on his face. He was blowing through the whistle I gave him earlier with all his toddler might, contributing his own bit of clamor to the moment. He stopped only for a second to smile at me from ear to tiny ear and I smiled right back. The air vibrated with the crowd's energy. For a moment, I marched absorbing the scene around me, letting the crowd carry me, and engraving the sights, sounds, and feelings into my memory.

It was an unusually warm November afternoon. At the end of our trek, on a lawn by City Hall, speakers addressed the crowd on a makeshift podium and less-than-perfect loudspeakers. They denounced any policy that draws legal conclusions along color lines, as Prop 187 did. Even the *paleteros* stopped pushing their ice cream carts for a while. We listened earnestly, absorbing the sense of community around us. Some people stood in groups, others sat on the packed lawn. Some found resting spots in the wide branches of the trees around us. Labeled buckets circulated the grounds, collecting money to support the cause that had brought us together. My eager fist raised itself repeatedly in support of the speakers, no longer the fist of an intimated child. After the speeches were through, we eventually headed home along the same route. Our strength had been seen and our voices had been heard loud and clear.

Unfortunately, most of us could not bring our message to the voting booths three weeks later. Many of us were not U.S. citizens yet. It could be years before all of us processed the papers that would grant us that power. On election night, I joined hundreds of volunteers at the Democratic headquarters at the Biltmore Hotel, watching in dismay as the votes rolled in. Californians passed Proposition 187 by a two-thirds majority vote. It was a hard loss, yet in the process, I began to recognize the true power of numbers.

Four months later, I had lunch with two friends at a Carl's Jr. Downtown, next to the Immigration Building on Los Angeles Street. The three of us worked together as environmental engineers for the City of Los Angeles. It was not obvious by looking at us, but Lisa, Dee, and I had more in common than I had with any of my former Spanish-haven classmates from Junior High or protest buddies from my militant phase in college, none of whom I kept in touch with anymore.

"So, what sorts of questions do you they ask during this citizenship test?" Lisa asked.

"Here," I said, handing her a list, "they have one hundred sample questions. They list the answers too, on the back."

They leaned in with curious eyes to browse the list. Dee was fascinated.

"What do the stripes on the flag mean? Are they serious?"

"Look at number 86," Lisa said, "Name one benefit of being a citizen of the United States."

They both looked at me, awaiting a response.

"Duh. To vote, of course."

They flipped to the back and looked puzzled.

"What? It's not ON there?" I yelled, making the entire fast-food lunch crowd come to a halt.

"Well, they only list three: Obtain Federal Government jobs; travel with a U.S. passport; and petition for close relatives to come to the U.S. to live."

"You've got to be kidding me," I said, snatching the list from them and searching frantically.

"To vote, to vote... okay, here it is. See? It's number 87: What is the MOST IMPORTANT right granted to citizens?" They looked relieved for me.

"They wouldn't ask anything that is not on the list, right?" Dee asked me.

"They're not supposed to, but that doesn't stop them. "

"How do you know?"

"When I went through the Amnesty Program five years ago, the man giving me the test decided the sample questions must be too easy for a 'UCLA Bruin'. He talked to me in a 'let's-see-how-smart-you-really-are' tone and an incredulous sneer. He asked me several names of my City and County representatives, plus the State senators, and seemed surprised that I named them all. Then, he wanted the name of the first female Justice in the Supreme Court. By that time, he had made me so nervous that Sandra Day O'Connor's name had completely escaped my brain."

Lisa and Dee felt my pain. To be stumped by a jerk on a power trip, and on <u>that</u> question, to make it worse.

I was not about to let that happen again, I told them. I had memorized that entire list. I even wrote extra questions that did not appear on the sample test: the name of every government official who represented me, the name of every Supreme Court justice...things that would surely stump the average, responsible, voting, American citizen. I just could not be too sure.

We finished our burgers and fries and not a moment too soon. My friends helped me check for mustard stains on my black and white suit, just as I said good-bye to them, and I rushed next door. I was only half an hour away from my U.S. citizenship interview.

"Are you gonna cooperate or are you gonna be a trouble maker?"

This is how the man behind the INS receptionist desk greeted me. I just stood there, contemplating his smirk, holding back my words. I had come too far and waited too long for this day to be distracted by anything petty.

"I have never been a trouble maker," I answered coldly and put my appointment slip in the empty tray.

The receptionist's grin was gone. He pointed out some forms I needed to complete before my appointment time. I grabbed the handful of duplicate color-coded papers from the desk, and scanned the room for a moment. There were about a hundred people scattered across the fourteen rows of seats. It was like an airport waiting room, with uncomfortable gray chairs packed too close together. The service counter housed the flags of California and the U.S. and a green Statue of Liberty. The statue's torch was visible above the maze of blue cubicles covering the rest of the office floor. I adjusted my jacket and headed into the room to find an empty spot.

The sound of my heels against the linoleum floor echoed in stereo.

The room was filled with faces of every color, most of them like mine. Some came with their children and others with their parents. Some looked exhausted, perhaps tired from fleeing the anti-immigrant hatred that chased them day in and day out. Some appeared to wait in distress, perhaps fearing they would never be forgiven the moral treason of renouncing their loyalty to their birthplace. Others waited with proud smiles, anxious to boast their new citizenship among U.S. admirers in their homelands. Many others wore a look of relief, ready to rid themselves of new "green card" expiration dates, renewal fees, and new deadlines for permanent residents. Others, like me, waited nervously to be granted the precious right to vote.

I sat down and began to look over the forms. I noticed something interesting at the bottom of the green one: two small boxes with the words "granted" and "denied" next to them. These tiny squares held my citizen status in less than a square centimeter. I stared at the squares in awe, and thought back a few weeks before.

I had asked some of my teenage cousins at a family gathering what they thought about "giving up" their Salvadoran citizenship. They, too, would one day be faced with the decision to become U.S. citizens, but their puzzled faces told me that they had never given it much thought. I had begun to realize how many of my own younger relatives would never struggle with this issue, being U.S. citizens by birth. They would probably take their birth right completely for granted. Maybe they would even misunderstand their history. At least, my cousins agreed that verbally "renouncing" their birth citizenship could never force anyone to renounce their birthrights or memories. I snapped back moments later, as I realized all of my forms were still blank.

Time dragged slowly as I waited for my turn. I double-checked my forms to make sure that they were perfect. I opened the manila envelope with the copy of my original application that I had with me, just in case. I read and re-read it. I pulled out my extra copy of the appointment slip I had placed in the tray at the counter to check my appointment time again.

"I should have made a copy of mine too, huh?" asked the man sitting next to me.

I did not know what to tell him.

While I waited, I looked up at the signs posted all over the sterile walls. No eating. No drinking. No smoking. No chewing gum. No loud noise. No visitors. Not even all the years I had spent going through bureaucracies helped to calm my nerves that day.

My interview time came and went and still no one called me in. I waited impatiently as I heard the people behind the counter reading out names. They spoke loudly and slowly as though our lack of citizenship made us incompetent somehow. Finally, forty-five minutes after my appointment time, an African-

American gentleman called me in. He directed me to his cubicle, where I swore to tell the truth, the whole truth, and nothing but the truth. He looked down and scribbled a few notes. His head was buried in a mountain of papers. Without looking up, he said I did not need to take a test because I had passed years before when receiving my permanent residence. He shuffled some more papers, stamped a few forms, casually marked the "granted" box on the green form, and held out his hand. He congratulated me with a tired smile and sent me on my way. I was done in just under three minutes.

Two months later I reported to the L.A. Convention Center to take my citizenship oath. I got out of my car and walked in with a large crowd. They came in, documents in hand, looking conspicuously nervous in their best Sunday clothes. A handful of ladies walked in wearing lace-covered evening gowns. A few gentlemen strolled along in tuxedo-like suits, proud as could be. I wore a dark green business suit and, despite the excessively formal attire around me, I felt quite overdressed. I wished I had worn something a bit more comfortable. I followed the crowd onto the escalator leading to the ballroom noted on my appointment sheet. I walked through the double doors at the top of the stairs and peeked inside past the multitude before me.

The hall was larger than a football field. Suspended from the high ceiling at the front, above the stage platform, was a huge U.S. flag. The draft from a nearby air conditioning vent made its corners flap lightly back and forth. The walkway was marked with worn velvet ropes. The roped path directed a river of people to the vacant seats on the left. A few solemn volunteers from a World War II Veteran group helped to guide the way. I smiled at the surprising number of elderly people going through the ceremony, many proudly waving the tiny plastic flags we found on our chairs. The Pilipino Veteran standing at the end of the aisle had thinning hair peeking from beneath his worn Garrison cap, and a reluctant smile revealed his hidden wrinkles. I stared, for a second, at the crooked lines across my face on my "Alien Registration Card" photo... that card was my livelihood, my right to exist, my most prized possession... the most important of my "papers." I had thought I might feel naked when asked to relinquish my card during the process. Instead, I felt free.

There were four thousand people there that morning. Four thousand more would come that afternoon. The judge strolled in wearing a long robe and a confidence that only years of officiating ceremonies like this can give. His hair was white with streaks of silver. Of the one hundred and eleven nations present that day, he said, the five countries most represented in this impressive crowd were, in order: Mexico, the Philippines, Vietnam, El Salvador, and Iran. My tiny El Salvador made the top five.

The terrorist bombing of the Federal Building in Oklahoma City, only days before, was fresh on everyone's minds. The judge realized that many of the people standing before him fled their countries to get away from precisely this kind of violence. Worried that this tragedy might appear as tolerance for terrorism on

America's part, he reassured us that we had made the right decision.

The hall was packed wall to wall with people. I surveyed the crowd but did not spot any of the images that the media would have the world believe about us. There were no illiterate peasants, no job-stealing "wetbacks," no lazy welfare mothers. There were no newlyweds married just for "papers," no anti-American segregationists, no terrorist extremists, no shameless tax dollar thieves. These "illegal alien" images often take our rightful place and speak for us, sneak into books, the news, the movies, television, and the minds of our peers, unbeknownst to us. Yet they were nowhere to be seen on the morning of my oath. There were only regular people from one hundred and eleven countries, wanting nothing else but to belong to this one.

Those alien images that follow me like shadows remain as distant from me as anything ever could be. Despite my different circumstances, my family's struggle was quite similar to every other family's. My family overcame obstacles through dedication and hard work — something most human beings do every day, no matter where they begin, where they end up, or what road they take to get there. I can only hope that my U.S.-born family will understand that they need not ever apologize for the place I have occupied. As have thousands like me, I eventually reached far beyond my underground life as an undocumented immigrant.

I sat through the citizenship ceremony, as a product of many things: of El Salvador's recent political history, of the Los Angeles Unified School District, of the University of California, of the "American" professional working culture, and most importantly, of my family's morals and values, where it all begins.

Back in El Salvador, my parents put food on the table for us three times a day. They eventually bought our first home and my sisters and I enrolled in private school. We were as "middle class" as middle class gets. We were blessed to be born in a living collage of emerald mountains, deep ravines, avocado groves, whispering creeks, open market places, small chicken farms, vast plantations, never-ending cotton fields, fragrant mango trees, dormant volcanoes, roads that go from paved to brick to dirt and back to paved again, and whole towns who know your name and your mother's name and her mother's name. There would not seem to be a reason good enough to abandon a place of such beauty, of such life.

But there were indeed motivations strong enough to make my family do just that. I know that each of the four thousand people who raised their right hands with me to repeat the citizenship oath that morning has a slightly different story. Many probably begin the same way, with vivid, youthful memories and a tremendous sense of loyalty to a birthplace left far behind. Sadly, many would rather forget the circumstances that may have brought them here. I certainly would not. The oath that is rejected by some has served as a reminder of my beginnings in El Salvador and of the nine days that brought my family to this country, inevitably and permanently changing my life.

.   .   .

The morning of my citizenship oath, I looked around the Convention Center floor once again as we were asked to raise our right hands. Looking over the hundreds of lifted heads before me, I recited that tricky oath – the one that goes unsaid and is taken for granted by so many every day.

"*I hereby declare, on oath, that I absolutely and entirely renounce and abjure all allegiance and fidelity to any foreign prince, potentate, state, or sovereignty, of whom or which I have heretofore been a subject or citizen; that I will support and defend the Constitution and laws of the United States of America against all enemies, foreign and domestic; that I will bear true faith and allegiance to the same; that I will bear arms on behalf of the United States when required by law; that I will perform noncombatant service in the armed forces when required by law; that I will perform work of national importance under civilian direction when required by law; and that I take this obligation freely without any mental reservation or purpose of evasion: So help me God.*"

Each person there had overcome obstacles. We were just as similar as we were unique. Perhaps some had dodged bullets in the rain long ago. Most had probably been ridiculed at some point over a nuance in their accent. Perhaps others had marched with me in East. L.A. just a few months before.

A perfect stillness overcame the crowded hall as we finished the last words of the oath. Even the corners of the U.S. flag above the stage seemed to have stopped flapping back and forth. For a moment, I was back in El Salvador, gazing over the rooftops of my sleeping hometown, contemplating our journey to the other side. I hardly sensed the roar of applause and cheers heard by the rest of the hall.

Amidst the commotion of the crowd and the echoes of storms past, I tried to concentrate in what lay ahead. The papers that had determined my fate for so many years no longer weighed me down. With my eyes closed and my hopes raised, I heard the distinct sound of my voice, growing stronger. And I smiled.

INFORMATION & RESOURCES

Information resources for and about undocumented immigrants (2008):

BACKGROUND INFORMATION

US Citizenship & Immigr. Services uscis.gov/graphics/shared/aboutus/statistics
U.S. Library of Congress   countrystudies.us/el-salvador/
Public Broadcasting System   pbs.org/wnet/justice/education/lp1.html

Excerpt from USCIS website: "*INS estimates that 7.0 million unauthorized immigrants resided in the United States in January 2000… States with the largest numerical increases in unauthorized population in the 1990s were California, Texas, Illinois, Arizona, Georgia, and North Carolina.*" In 2006, the Public Policy Institute of CA estimated the undocumented immigrant population at **11.5 million**, growing at about 500,00 per year (www.ppic.org)

RESOURCES & SUPPORT

Central American Resource Center	(213) 385-7800	www.carecen-la.org
Mex-American Legal Defense Educ Fund	(213) 629-2512	www.maldef.org
California Immigrant Welfare Collaborative	(916) 448-6762	www.nilc.org/ciwc
National Council of La Raza	(202) 785-1670	www.nclr.org
AZ: Florence Immigrant&Refugee Rights	(520) 868-0191	www.firrp.org
CA: ACLU Immigrant Rights Project	(510) 625-2010	www. aclu.org
GA: Office of Civil Rights (Atlanta)	(404) 562-7886	www.hhs.gov/ocr
IL: Midwest Immig & Human Rights Ctr	(312) 660-1300	www.heartlandalliance.org/mihrc
FL: Florida Immigrant Advocacy Center	(305) 573-1106	www.fiacfla.org
NC: Immigrant Legal Assistance Project	(888) 251-2776	www.ncjustice.org/ilap
NY: ACLU Immigrant Rights Project	(212) 549-2660	www. aclu.org
TX: Catholic Charities (Houston)	(713) 526-4611	www.catholiccharities.org
WA: Northwest Immigrant Rights Project	(509) 854-2100	www.lawhelp.org

ANTI-IMMIGRANT LEGISLATION

Legislation to ban public benefits for undocumented immigrants has been passed or is being pursued in many states. Some state courts have found such legislation unconstitutional, but the U.S. Supreme Court has yet to rule on the topic. Search Internet under "*undocumented immigrant benefit ban*". Examples:

11/1994 California Proposition 187: Banned public services for undocumented immigrants, allows questioning of anyone "reasonably suspicious". Requires police, doctors, teachers & other public employees to report undoc. immigrants. STATUS: Overturned in Federal Court 1995 (deemed unconstitutional).

02/2005 Georgia HR-256: Calls for a state constitutional amendment to ban all public services to undoc. immigrants including all publicly funded healthcare and all education, including K-12. STATUS: Stalled on GA House floor in early 2005.

02/2005 The REAL ID Act (H.R. 418): Prohibits states from issuing driver's licenses to undoc. immigrants; makes people deportable for First Amendment-protected activity; eliminates environmental & other laws to allow completion of fence along US/Mexico border. STATUS: passed House in 2005; died in Senate

12/2005 "Securing America's Borders" (H.R. 4437): Makes it a felony to enter the US without documents and criminalizes individuals who offer assistance. Triggered **a historic series of immigrant rights demonstrations** nationwide, starting in March 2006. STATUS: House passed HR4437 in 12/2005. Senate's less severe version of the bill (S.2611) died on the Senate floor in 2006.

EDUCATION
Legislation – Access to Elementary & Secondary Education
Right for all children to attend school: Plyler V. Doe, 457 U.S. 202 (1982)

Limitations on residency inquiries: Plyler v. Doe, 457 U.S. 202 (1982); Horton v. Marshall Public Schools, 769 E2D 1323 (8th. Cir. 1985); Byrd v. Livingston School District, 674 ESupp. 225 (E.D. Texas 1987); Martinez v. Bynum, 461 U.S. 321 (1983) upholding a legitimate residency request.

Right to see records and to keep records confidential: 20USC1232(g) (also known as the Family Educational Rights and Privacy Act "FERPA" or Buckley Amendment) et. seq.

Legislation – Access to Higher Education
1985 Leticia A. v. Board of Regents, No. 588982-4 (Superior Court, County of Alameda, May 7, 1985). California Education Code § 68062(h) - allowed undocumented students to attend college and pay in-state tuition fees, and qualify for need-based financial aid.

1990 Regents of UC v. Superior Court (Bradford) 225 Cal.App.3d 972, *reh. den. (1991)*: Overturned California's Leticia A. Ruling. Requires newly enrolled undocumented students to be considered non-residents for tuition purposes. Adopted by UC and by community colleges in 1991 and by CSU campuses in 1996.

2002 CA Assembly Bill 540 (AB540). Allows undocumented students to attend CA public colleges and pay in-state tuition fees if: they attended a CA high school for 3 or more years; graduated from a CA high school; register or be currently enrolled in a CA Community College, Cal State, or a University of California; sign a statement with the college or university (NOT with INS) stating that he/she will apply for legal residency as soon as he/she is eligible to do so. Other states that have enacted legislation similar to AB540 include: Illinois, New Mexico, Oklahoma, Utah, Kansas, Nebraska, New York, Texas and Washington (www.maldef.org/ab540/pdf/ab540.brochure.pdf)

2005 Development Relief and Education for Alien Minors Act ("DREAM Act" U.S. Senate Bill 1545), if enacted, would facilitate state efforts to offer in-state tuition to undocumented students. Along with the "Student Adjustment Act" (House Resolution 1684), the DREAM Act would allow hardworking immigrant youth who have long resided in the U.S., the chance to adjust their status after meeting certain conditions. STATUS: Both measures were introduced but <u>not passed</u> in 2004, 2005 and 2007. The DREAM Act may be re-visited following the HISTORIC 2008 Presidential Election (www.nclr.org)

Scholarships
See MALDEF website or search the Internet under "*scholarship undocumented student*" to find scholarships available to students regardless of immigration status (www.maldef.org/pdf/Scholarships_072004.pdf). MALDEF website excerpt:

"*In order to qualify for state and federal financial aid, students must be permanent legal residents or citizens. The scholarships on this list do not require a social security number, legal residency, or citizenship. As a general rule, if an application asks for your social security number and you do not have one yet, leave that space blank but fill out and turn in the application. Lying about your legal status or providing a false social security is a federal offense*".

DISASTER ASSISTANCE
Adapted from Federal Emergency Management Agency (FEMA) (800) 621-3362 website News Release 06/17/2004 (www.fema.gov):

After a natural disaster, immigrants may be eligible for some services: crisis counseling; disaster legal services; other short-term, non-cash, emergency aid; and cash assistance for minor child under 18 years of age. If you don't qualify, FEMA can refer you to other assistance programs. Some state/local agencies may offer cash assistance to undocumented immigrants in the event of a natural disaster. Contact American Red Cross (866) 438-4636 (English), (800) 257-7575 (Spanish)

TE PRESTO UN ESPEJO

Para mi hija, mis sobrinos, mis primos, y cualquier otro
chiquitín nacido fuera de nuestra Tierra, El Salvador.

Prestame tus ojos y yo te presto el pasado
Para que algún día entendás tu presente y tu futuro.
Porqué crecés en tierra ajena, y aunque no te des cuenta
Tu raíz esta sembrada en otro lado,
Donde todo es igual y distinto al mismo tiempo.

Aquel muchacho en las noticias, va corriendo de la migra, huyendo,
Lleno de miedo y de valor. Anda escondido en las sombras,
En los arbustos del desierto, en un baúl oscuro,
En un apartamento repleto... Que no te sorprenda lo que hace.
Quizá por el mismo camino han venido tus abuelos, o tu vecino,
O hasta tu mejor amigo.
Ese muchacho que corta lechuga para tu hamburguesa,
Que lava tus platos, que sirve tu pizza,
Que barre tu escuela, y te vende naranjas,
Ese muchacho con el acento que te ofende el oído,
Fijate bien en su apellido – que puede ser el tuyo ó el mío.

Aquella cipota que no haz conocido juega con una llanta vieja
que halló en un barranco hecho basurero –
Empezó a vender en el mercado antes de empezar el tercer grado.
Talvez nunce se queje por deberes escolares
Ni tenga cuaderno donde escribir su nombre.
Esa niña de piel morena y pies descalzos
A veces alegre, a veces callada,
Con la sonrisa triste y el alma cansada, tan temprano.
Se entretiene en sus cumpleaños, saltando hule,
Sin pastel, ni candelas que apagar. Dejará de ser niña
sin tener muñeca, ni regalo de navidad, mucho menos Playstation.
Pudiste ser ella y ella pudo ser vos. Y sí lo es.

Aquel viejito de sangre indígena
Que se mueve despacio entre los volcanes y el tiempo,
Se aleja sonriente del apuro moderno
Sin conocer el avión, ni la tele, mucho menos e-mail.
Ese anciano con sombrero de paja
Lleva sandalias de cuero cubiertas de cansancio,
Se viste de arrugas y de piel tostadita
por los años trabajando bajo el sol.
Con cada paso se hace parte del paisaje
que solo has visto en tarjetas postales
ó en la pared de la pupusería local.
Vive vida simple, el viejito, sin lujos,
Todo lo que necesita lo lleva consigo.
Más que todo, la paz con si mismo.

Aquella señora que ves todas las mañanas
Esperando el bus en la parada de la esquina,
Todavía se confunde con las monedas nuevas.
Está recién llegada de otra parte, donde no era todo tan extraño.
Donde ha dejado a sus hijos y a su razón de ser,
Pues por forjarles un futuro, sacrifica su presente.
Esa señora no maneja, no conoce días feriados, ni vestidos nuevos,
mucho menos Yoga. Sola en las noches, saca las fotos de sus niños
Tratando de que no les caigan lágrimas.
Con la mano que recibió diploma restrega la tina de la dueña,
Así sale adelante con pasos atrás
Y guarda el recuerdo de su carrera y sus sueños.
La única carrera que le queda es entre Trader Joe's y Starbucks
Haciendo mandados para sus jefes.
Esa señora humilde que limpia tu casa y cose tu ropa,
que cocina tu almuerzo y cría a tus amigos,
Tiene el rostro de tu prima, de tu tía, y de tu madre,
Que no te de lástima – talvez en su presente hay más orgullo
De lo que aparienta.

Prestame tus oídos y yo te presto el eco
De cascadas antiguas en selvas vírgenes
De grillos susurrando por las madrugadas
De himnos solemnes de Semana Santa
De cumbias alegres en fiestas de Oriente
De un buey pasando por vereda adoquinada
De vendedoras gritando en mercados al aire
De cuetes anunciando Navidad y Año Nuevo
De huevos chimbos reventándose de risa
Asomate a la ventana y escuchá la serenata
Que te canta el pasado y el presente,
Y verás con el alma lo que solo te han contado...
Los campos empapados de sudor y de lluvia,
los pueblos enteros borrados por la guerra
y talvez tambien a esa señora humilde,
a ese viejito sonriente, a esa cipota triste,
a ese muchacho huyendo...
Talvez verás que ellos llevarán tu rostro
Y vos el de ellos, por siempre.

Prestame un momento y yo te presto un cuento
Y el recuerdo de un hogar que atraviesa el tiempo
Y una hamaca que te arrulle hasta que amanezca
Para que soñés con la herencia que te da tu origen.
Y para que veás lo lindo, lo duro, y lo cierto
De cerca y de lejos, con este espejo que te presto.

Evelyn Cortez-Davis - noviembre 2001

I'LL LEND YOU A MIRROR

*For my daughter, my nephews, my cousins, and any other
little one born outside our homeland, El Salvador.*

Lend me your eyes and I will lend you the past
So at last you can grasp your today and tomorrow
Because you grow far from home while you may not realize
That your essence is rooted someplace else
Where all is different, yet somehow is all the same.

That young man on the news, running from *La Migra* –
He flees, full of fear and of courage. He hides in the shadows,
In the desert brush, in the trunk of a Buick, in a crowded apartment...
Do not be surprised by his choices or by the silent voices
Of your neighbors and your not-so-distant relatives
Who used that same old road to their American Dream.
That young man who cleans your dishes, serves your pizza,
Sweeps your school, and sells you oranges – turning invisible before your eyes.
That young man who cuts the lettuce for your burger works to go further
Than generations before him -- as you look away and ignore him.
He smiles with pride for having any work at all.
That young man with the accent that offends you,
Pay attention to his name: it might be the same as one closer than you think.

That young *cipota* you will never meet
Plays with an old tire she found in a ravine full of trash
She has been selling at the market since before the third grade
She will never complain of too much homework
Or have a notebook to practice her name.
The girl with the cinnamon skin and dusty bare feet has eyes that rejoice
With simple pleasures like gulping grape soda or jumping over puddles,
Her dimples don't reveal her tired little soul,
A smile so young, and already so grown.
She will frolic on her birthdays with a make-shift jumprope,
Without candles on a cake, or wishes to make, or hope.
She will grow out of her childhood without dolls, or an allowance,
Or Christmas presents, or Playstation.
She could have been you and you could have been her. And you are.

Can you see that brave old man, so distant from your life?
He strolls serenely through awakened volcanoes,
With your ancestors' blood flows through his veins
And the dignity of the harvest engraved in his back.
Patiently, he walks away from the haste and modern hype
He has never known the airplane, or e-mail, or HDTV.
He is dressed in wrinkles and fatigue and a straw hat full of holes,
His shoulders toasted by the years in the cotton fields.
With each step he blends into the cobblestone paths,
He becomes the coconut trees, the hibiscus blooms,
And the emeralds crowning the jagged hills.
He lives a simple life, without luxury, or greed...
All he needs, the old man carries with him, above all, inner peace.

That lady you see in the mornings waiting at the corner for the bus,
Counts her fare and gets confused with coins she's never used.
She's just arrived from far away, where all was not so strange,
Where she has left her *retoñitos*, her reason for being,
And to forge for them a tomorrow, she throws away her today.
That woman has no car, or make-up,
She does not know cell phones, or holidays,
Or new dresses, much less Yoga.
Alone at night, she holds a picture, shielding it from her tears.
She touches her children's faces and imagines them here,
They will forget her voice through the years, she fears.
The same hand that held her diploma
Scrubs the tub that someone else enjoys.
So she dreams and scrubs, scrubs and dreams of a career that cannot be.
That humble woman whom you pity, who raises your children,
Cooks your dinner, sews your clothes, and does your laundry -
She looks like your cousin, your aunt, and your mother,
You see her waiting on the corner, with more pride than she reveals,
She will still move ahead, even with steps back
And you wonder if your will can ever equal hers.

Listen to the echoes that the miles have kept from you,
Of ancient waterfalls in pristine jungles,
And crickets humming before sunrise,
Merchants' screams in open markets,
Bursts of laughter, confetti eggs cracking,
Cuetes announcing the New Year,
Noisy wagons pulled by oxen,
Solemn hymns at Easter masses,
And rhythmic *cumbias* at small town dances...
Peek through your window and listen
To the serenade of your past and your present
And you will sample the delights of your inheritance
And see with your soul what you have only heard of...
Coffee fields drenched with sweat and rain,
Entire villages erased by war,
And perhaps you'll also see
The humble lady counting coins,
The calm *viejito* strolling by,
The little girl with the grown-up soul,
The young man with the proud smile...
Perhaps you will see that they wear your face
And you, theirs - always.

Lend me a moment so you can see the mirror in my words
And I will lend you the memory of a home that does not fade
And a hammock to rock you until the sun rises again
So you may dream of the place that is yours,
Where all seems so different, yet somehow is always the same.

Evelyn Cortez-Davis – November 2001

ACKNOWLEDGEMENTS

First and foremost, I thank God for blessing my life more than I could ever dream. I would like to thank my family and friends for allowing me to tell my memories as I remember them. I have taken creative liberty to recreate conversations to capture feelings based my recollection or accounts of others. In many cases, names outside of my immediate family have been changed.

I thank my husband and best friend, Troy J. Davis for encouraging me to sit down and write, and our daughter Dakota for motivating me to finish. For their unconditional support, I thank my parents, Juan and Rosario Cortez; my amazing sisters, Sonia Cortez, Milady Medina, and Daysi Cortez Hernandez, and their families; my incredible grandmothers, Aurora Grande and Lidia Santos; my grandfathers Jerónimo Grande and José Ursulo Cortez, who will always be always with us; my Tios Edgardo Palencia and Donel Chicas for helping us to learn English - I miss you both greatly. For her unwavering support of our family through the years, I thank our friend Bertha Lopez. For their patience through my many interviews and readings for my project, I thank my extended family: the Cortez, Davis, Santos, Grande, Hernandez, Argueta, Medina, Robinson, Maso-Soto, Myles, Baldridge, Jacobs, Palencia, Gavidia, and Lopez Families.

For influencing my life more than they realize, I thank my teachers and mentors: Ms. Lee, Mr. Lehman, and Mr. Gherardi from Columbus Junior High School; Mrs. Anna Cohen from Canoga Park High School; and Thomas Donohoe and Sherry Hormozi from UCLA.

For their invaluable editorial insight that helped me shape my story, I thank my friends and avid supporters: Charisse Meigs Stewart, Dee Beingessner, Lisa Mowery, Salvador Ledezma, and Dr. Horacio N. Roque-Ramirez.

RECONOCIMIENTOS

En primer lugar, le agradezco a Dios por bendecir mi vida mas de lo que podría soñar. Quisiera agradecerles a mis familiares y amigos por permitirme contar mis relatos tal como yo los recuerdo. Me he permitido la libertad creativa de recrear conversaciones para capturar sentimientos, basadas en mi propia memoria y en los recuerdos de otros. En muchos casos, los nombres fuera de mi familia inmediata han sido cambiados.

Le agradezco a mi esposo y mejor amigo, Troy J. Davis por animarme a que me sentara y escribiera, y a nuestra hija Dakota, por motivarme para que terminara. Por su apoyo incondicional, les agradezco a mis padres, Juan y Rosario Cortez; a mis increíbles hermanas, Sonia Cortez, Milady Medina, y Daysi Cortez Hernandez, y sus familias; a mis maravillosas abuelas, Aurora Grande y Lidia Santos; a mis abuelos Jerónimo Grande y José Ursulo Cortez, quienes siempre estarán con nosotros; a mis Tios Edgardo Palencia y Donel Chicas por ayudarnos a aprender Inglés – los extraño a los dos tremendamente. Por su apoyo constante através de los años, le doy las gracias a nuestra amiga, Bertha López. Por su paciencia durante mis repetidas entrevistas y lecturas para mi proyecto, le agradezco a mi familia extendida: las Familias Cortez, Davis, Santos, Grande, Hernandez, Argueta, Medina, Robinson, Maso-Soto, Myles, Baldridge, Jacobs, Palencia, Gavidia, y Lopez.

Por influir en mi vida más de lo que se dan cuenta, les doy las gracias a mis maestros y mentores: Srita. Lee, Sr. Lehman, y Sr. Gherardi de Columbus Junior High School; Sra. Anna Cohen de Canoga Park High School; y Thomas Donohoe y Sherry Hormozi de UCLA.

Por su respaldo e inestimable perspicacia editorial que me ayudó a realizar mi historia, doy gracias a mis amigos: Charisse Meigs Stewart, Dee Beingessner, Lisa Mowery, Salvador Ledezma, y el Dr. Horacio N. Roque-Ramirez.